CONTENTS

Ships in Focus Publications

Correspondence and editorial:
Roy Fenton
18 Durrington Avenue
London SW20 8NT
020 8879 3527
rfenton@rfenton.demon.co.uk

Orders and photographic:
John & Marion Clarkson
18 Franklands, Longton
Preston PR4 5PD
01772 612855
shipsinfocus@btinternet.com

Printed by Amadeus Press Ltd.,
Cleckheaton, Yorkshire.
Designed by Hugh Smallwood, John Clarkson
and Roy Fenton.

SHIPS IN FOCUS RECORD
ISBN 978-1-901703-99-3

SUBSCRIPTION RATES FOR RECORD

Readers can start their subscription with any
issue, and are welcome to backdate it to receive
previous issues.

	3 issues	4 issues
UK	£24	£31
Europe (airmail)	£26	£34
Rest of the world (surface mail)	£26	£34
Rest of the world (airmail)	£31	£41

On the page opposite is an announcement of the latest book from Ships in Focus. The subject, Cunard Line, may be somewhat surprising, but together with author Peter Newall we believe this book will come to be regarded as the definitive fleet history of this famous company. None of the many other books on Cunard presents such a comprehensive picture of its activities, including histories of its services and all its many ships, the majority of which are illustrated. The focus is not just on the transatlantic passenger liners, although they get their fair share of exposure. Covered in similar depth are the intermediate passenger ships, Mediterranean traders, the surprisingly large fleet of pure cargo ships, Cunard's contribution to the Atlantic Container Line, reefers, cruise ships, the bulkers of Cunard-Brocklebank, the Moss tankers plus tugs and tenders. Then there is the impressive fleet of wartime managed ships, including some famous foreign liners. Coasters and other ships chartered for Channel Islands and Great Lakes services are also mentioned. Whatever your interest in ships, you will find much to enjoy, and the fleet listings reflect the latest standards of research with details from registration papers and other sources. Production is being finalised as this editorial is written, and we expect to despatch orders in January.

Those in the UK will be well aware of the recent swingeing increases in postal rates (undoubtedly a prelude to privatisation of the Royal Mail), far out of proportion to any increase in personal incomes which all but city bankers can expect. With even a domestic second class letter costing 50p (that's ten shillings in old money) Ships in Focus regrets that it will not be sending out Christmas cards this year, and we would encourage others to adopt similar economies. Nevertheless, in this the last 'Record' of 2012, we would like to thank all our contributors and readers for their support and wish them well for Christmas and the New Year.

This issue has more than a flavour of the antipodean, with Ian Farquhar's feature on Melbourne photographer Allan Green and Andrew Bell's on British Phosphate Commissioners. The latter is a fascinating story which encompasses not just ships, but geology, agriculture, politics, wartime conflict, greed and profligacy. We also have a posthumous article by Graeme Somner, whose obituary appears in 'Bosun's Locker'. 'Putting the Record straight' in this issue is one of the longest we have ever run, and we continue to be grateful to the many readers who provide letters and e-mails concerning past articles.

This is reminder that the London-based editor has had severe e-mail problems recently, and we apologise if any contributor's or reader's communication has not been acknowledged. In an effort to resolve the problems, there is a new editorial e-mail address, record@rfenton.co.uk which please use from now on.

John Clarkson
Roy Fenton

Nauru Chief was purchased from London owners in 1921: see page 42.
[State Library of Victoria, H91.325 1177]

ESKDENE

Originally founded in Cardiff in 1932 as the Dene Shipmanagement Co. Ltd., what was to later become the Dene Shipping Co. Ltd. quickly set about forming a number of single-ship subsidiaries, operated in a fleet which was to establish, and maintain, a long new building connection with West Hartlepool shipbuilder William Gray. By 1936 the companies had moved to London, adding a number of shipping personalities from West Hartlepool to the board of directors on the way. In this way came an involvement with the Barraclough family and eventually with Silver Line, culminating in control of that company.

Eskdene was unfortunate to suffer damage by mine or submarine attack just three months after war broke out on the 2nd December 1939. Carrying a cargo of timber, she was some 70 miles north east of the River Tyne entrance, listing heavily to starboard and down by the stern, when two Tyne tugs made contact and successfully brought the stricken vessel to the river and beached her on the Herd Sands, South Shields, the designated wartime emergency beaching ground, where what remained of her cargo was removed. *Eskdene* was later refloated, repaired, and returned to service, only to succumb to a torpedo attack in the North Atlantic on the 6th March 1941. *[W. Parry and Sons Ltd./ Author's collection]*

NAILSEA COURT

Bartram's version of the 'new era' tramp was a vessel with dimensions 420.3 x 56.0 x 25.4 feet, configured to the complete superstructure design with forecastle, and a midship superstructure split by number 3 hold, with numbers 1 and 2 holds forward and 4 and 5 aft of the structure. As noted elsewhere, she was fitted with a White compound engine built at Hebburn-on-Tyne. As White did not have installation facilities of his own, he had to use those of other engine builders, in this case George Clark at Southwick, Sunderland. *Nailsea Court's* maiden voyage commenced on the 17th August 1936, and took her to Panama, probably for further orders. On the 19th March 1943 she became one of the 27 'Scrap and Build' vessels to be lost by enemy action when torpedoed in the North Atlantic. *[W. Parry and Sons Ltd./Author's collection]*

BARTRAM TRAMPS OF THE THIRTIES
John Lingwood

With the First World War at an end, 1919 started off as a boom year for British shipping and, with the expectation of excellent returns, ship owners rushed to place orders for new ships which shipbuilders were only too happy to accept, given the unprecedented prices they were able to quote. But the boom did not last and by the mid-twenties the bubble had burst leaving many owners and builders in financial ruin.

It was the beginning of a sequence of 'boom and bust' for all sections of the British shipping industry which was to continue for close on twenty years, encompassing the worldwide depression years of the 'thirties. Ports, rivers and harbours were filled with laid-up ships and most shipyards experienced long periods of idleness and, in too many cases, complete closure.

Bartrams' survival strategy

Sunderland shipbuilder Bartram and Sons was one of the companies which managed to survive these desperate times by picking up the odd order here and there, indulging in some shipbreaking, and even manufacturing luxury caravans for those who, despite the depression, had the wherewithal to go off on touring holidays. Thanks to this diversification the yard was able to keep a nucleus of technical staff and apprentices in employment, putting some to use in the drawing office progressing new ideas for improving the design and efficiency of the cargo ship of the day.

Faced with a similar dearth of orders in 1922, the company had built an oil tanker as a speculation in the hope of encouraging further work and, despite the failure of that ploy (the vessel went straight into lay-up for two years before being bought by Newcastle owners and given the name *Malistan*), they now decided to try the tactic again, choosing this time to lay the keel in 1930 of hull number 271, a single-deck, full-scantling tramp ship configured with poop, bridge and forecastle erections. The midships bridge was of the 'long' variety, leaving short wells forward and aft over numbers one and four holds, and providing additional cargo space in the bridge 'tween deck built over numbers two and three holds, a layout favoured by many owners working in the grain trades, particularly where 'parcels' of cargo were loaded for delivery at various ports.

It should be noted that, with this design, the single deck formed the 'uppermost continuous deck', and was also the freeboard and tonnage deck. Vessels were therefore assigned the maximum draught and corresponding maximum deadweight but, on the other hand, gross, net and under deck tonnages were also maximum, resulting in high port dues and expenses.

With principal dimensions of 371.0 x 51.5 x 22.4 feet and a deadweight of 6,680 tons on a draft of 22 feet 1½ inches, the vessel's design and specification followed very closely that of the then current 'Fairplay Standard Ship'. That authoritative shipping magazine specialised in matters of maritime finance, and regularly published estimates of building costs for a theoretical, typical cargo ship design of the day, which served as a yardstick of current trends. In fact hull number 271, which was fitted with a triple-expansion engine built by John Dickinson and Sons Ltd. of Sunderland,

went beyond the 'Fairplay' basis and incorporated some of the new ideas worked on, as described above, by Bartram's skeleton design staff, notably modified aft-end hull lines aimed at improving the flow of water to a propeller designed in conjunction with the National Physical Laboratory at Teddington. Also included was a streamlined, aerofoil-shaped, semi-balanced rudder, integral with a more efficient stern frame and rudder post. These were features which were to be incorporated into most of the company's cargo ship designs for decades to come. However, of more significance was the fact that whereas the 'Fairplay' ship was specified to attain a service speed of 9 knots on 25 tons of coal per day, the Bartram ship reached that speed on just 11 tons per day - justification for the hard work carried out behind the scenes in the otherwise idle drawing office.

Once again Bartram's plan proved unsuccessful and, by the time the vessel neared completion in 1931, no buyer had been found; in fact, it was to be three more years before she was bought by the newly formed Dene Ship Management Company, and launched on the 10th September 1934 as *Eskdene* for their subsidiary Eskdene Shipping Co. Ltd. Just one month later on the 13th October, she was captured on camera by South Shields marine photographer W. Parry and Son Ltd., on loaded sea trials prior to sailing away on her maiden voyage to Oran with a cargo of coal. As the photograph shows, the vessel's appearance was little changed from that in vogue since the early twentieth century, with tall, stove-pipe funnel, counter stern and vertical, flat bar stem. Little did Parry and Sons know, but they were photographing a ship which would mark the end of an era of tramp ship design.

Post-depression design

If Bartrams expected Dene's decision to buy their new ship would immediately encourage other owners to follow suit, they were to be disappointed, for it was to be almost two years before another new vessel was completed at the South Dock shipyard. Named *Nailsea Court* when launched on 9th June 1936, hull number 272 was the first of four sisters ordered by the E.R. Management Company of Cardiff, part of the Evans and Reid Group, and placed, two each, in the ownership of their subsidiaries Nailsea Steam Ship Co. Ltd. and Bantham Steam Ship Co. Ltd. The incentive for owners to place orders at this time came largely from the implementation by the British Government of their 1935 British Shipping (Assistance) Act, part II of which became more commonly known as 'Scrap and Build', since loans for modernisation of fleets were initially available on the basis of scrapping one gross ton for every ton modernised.

Nailsea Court was a Bantham ship, and she was followed into that fleet by hull number 274, named *Nailsea Meadow* when launched on the 18th December 1936 (after five attempts to launch her into the North Sea had been cancelled due to high winds), whilst *Nailsea Moor* and *Nailsea Manor*, hull numbers 276 and 277, were launched on the 12th June and 21st September 1937, respectively, for the Nailsea company. Filling the gaps between the Nailsea ships were two vessels built for another Cardiff owner,

NAILSEA MANOR

Founded in 1880, the Evans and Reid company rapidly became established as one of the leading Cardiff coal exporting businesses with customers including the Royal Navy and railway companies worldwide. In 1932 they formed the first of two shipping companies, purchasing second-hand vessels to carry their own coal to these markets, and were amongst the first to make use of the 'Scrap and Build' facilities, acquiring a dozen or more vessels which were scrapped as part of the deal which enabled the Bartram vessels to be built. The photographs of *Nailsea Court* and *Nailsea Manor* illustrate the alternative funnel markings used by the two owning companies (it is also interesting to note that the two Bantham newbuildings had teak bulwarks at two levels of the bridge front whilst the Nailsea ships had only one). *Nailsea Manor*, which had her White compound engine fitted at John Dickinson's Sunderland engine works, became a war loss on the 10th of October 1941. *[W. Parry and Sons Ltd./Author's collection]*

old customer Evan Thomas, Radcliffe (ETR), which took delivery of hulls 273 and 275, *Llanashe* and *Llandaff,* in November 1936 and May 1937. Only *Nailsea Moor* and *Llandaff* of this sextet survived the Second World War and, coincidentally, they were to come together following the acquisition in 1947 by the Evans and Reid Group of ETR, which had been experiencing difficulties looking elsewhere for freight, following the collapse of their staple coal trade.

In all, Bartrams built ten ships (not eleven as stated in my article in 'Record' 50) to this 'post-thirties depression' design between 1936 and 1938. Although it was largely the financial assistance available from 'Scrap and Build' which had sparked the influx of orders into British shipyards in the mid-thirties, only the four Nailsea ships benefited from this section of the British Shipping Act: *Nailsea Moor's* building cost of £89,645 was aided by a loan of £88,625; *Nailsea Manor's* loan covered the full building cost of £94,300: *Nailsea Court* received £77,340 against a cost of £82,300 and *Nailsea Meadow* £74,655/£82,950.

It should also be noted that two more vessels, *Harpagus* (hull 282) and *Harpalyce* (283), were delivered after the outbreak of the Second World War to a design modified from the 'Nailsea' ships to suit Admiralty requirements (see 'Record 50' and Malcolm Cooper's 'J. and C. Harrison: the History of a Family Shipping Venture'), and for which their owner J. and C. Harrison received financial grants, whilst two more, *Richmond Hill* (hull 284) and *Pentridge Hill* (285) were built for the British flag subsidiary of Rethymnis and Kulukundis, Counties Ship Management, to an Isherwood 'Arcform' design, and received loans under the later, Shipping Loan agreement.

The Evan Thomas, Radcliffe duo *Llanashe* and *Llandaff*, together with two vessels for Greek owners S.G. Embiricos and N.G. Nicolaou named *Ellin* (hull 278), and *Agios Georgios IV* (279) respectively, the *Lodestone* (280) built for the Alva Steamship Company of London, and *Suva* (281) built for the Anglo-Australian trading company W.R. Carpenter and Company, completed the tally of ships built to the 'Nailsea' design. However, these were all ordered by their owners on the perception that freight rates were improving and were financed without government aid. The roller-coaster years of the 'twenties and early 'thirties had drawn to a close with the five years up to 1934 regarded as being the worst for world trade yet experienced, and were made worse for shipping by the failure of the Argentine wheat crop in the winter of 1934. This had resulted in a lack of orders for the shipment of grain to Europe, so essential to the trading pattern of most tramp ship owners, with many vessels waiting in the River Plate for orders which did not come. Eventually British and Greek ship owners came together to find a solution to this problem, and thrashed out a minimum freight rate for these cargoes. This sparked off a general improvement in rates which were to hold firm until the outbreak of the Second World War.

Worldwide economic recovery is generally regarded as having its beginning in 1934, with shipping starting to feel benefits over the next two years as noted above. The Bartram shipyard, of course, had not been the only British shipyard to put its unused managers and apprentices to work, in conjunction with the much improved technical assistance now becoming available from the tank testing establishments and universities, on designs for new and more efficient cargo ships and, in all, some 17 other shipbuilders which had managed to survive the depression joined with the South Dock yard to herald in a new era of tramp ship design.

LLANASHE and LLANDAFF

Evan Thomas and Henry Radcliffe
had come together in 1882 to form a
shipping company whose fortunes,
prior to the Second World War, were
based almost entirely on the Cardiff
coal trade. Following the death of
Evan Thomas in 1891, the Radcliffe
family carried on the business, building
up a large fleet of tramp ships, mostly
registered in the ownership of single
ship companies (at one time as many
as 31 of these had been formed).
Bartram's first built for Evan Thomas,
Radcliffe (ETR) in 1924, and the
association was continued in 1952
when the motor vessel *Llantrisant*
became the first UK flag vessel to
be ordered and built by the shipyard
post-war, following a long run of export
orders. By now part of the Evans and
Reid Group, the company continued in
the tramping trade, but also expanded
into the tanker market, and even
operated two coasters in its last years.

Although built to the 'Nailsea'
design, *Llanashe* and *Llandaff* did
differ from the Evans and Reid
vessels in so far as neither had a
forecastle erection, and the midship
superstructure was modified. The
White engines of both vessels were
installed at George Clark's works.
Llanashe (seen arriving at Cape Town
on her maiden voyage and also at
Avonmouth) was torpedoed and sunk
on the 23rd August 1943, but her
sister survived the war to be sold by
ETR in 1951 and ending her days
in a breakers' yard in 1959 after a
grounding. *[Roy Fenton collection;J.
and M. Clarkson; Tom Rayner/J. and
M. Clarkson]*

AGIOS GEORGIOS IV

Bartram and Sons first built for a Greek owner, Stathatos Brothers, in 1877 and later added to their list of customers Vagliano Brothers, regarded by many as the founders of the London Greek community. After a long gap the Greek connection was resumed when S.G. Embiricos took delivery of *Ellin* in 1937, followed by *Agios Georgios IV*, photographed by Parry on a successful trial on the 6th July 1938 when she attained a speed of 11 knots, before acceptance into the Piraeus-based fleet of N.G. Nicolaou. Whilst *Ellin* was fitted with a North Eastern Marine triple-expansion engine, *Agios Georgios IV* had a White compound engine fitted at John Dickinson's Monkwearmouth engine works on the River Wear at Sunderland. Her main difference from other vessels of the 'Nailsea' design was the addition of a teak-faced flying bridge above the wheel house. *Agios Georgios IV* became a war loss on 8th June 1942 when she was sunk by gunfire from a Japanese submarine off Madagascar. *[W. Parry and Sons Ltd./Author's collection]*

LODESTONE

Bartram's yard number 280, *Lodestone* was one of three similar-sized cargo vessels built in the UK during 1938 for the Alva Steamship Co. Ltd, one of two companies set up in London that year by Andre Vlasov. A Russian émigré, he had left his native country in 1917 and settled in Roumania where he set up companies involved in the sale of Polish coal to countries throughout the Eastern Mediterranean, eventually acquiring his own ships for use in this trade. In 1934 he expanded his business into Greece and, in 1937, the United Kingdom, where he became involved with Manuel Kulukundis of the influential Rethymnis and Kulukundis shipping group, setting up the Campden Hill Steamship Company within their Counties Ship Management organisation. Manuel Kulukundis was also involved in the ordering of the three Alva newbuildings. A revolution in Roumania saw Andre Vlasov move to Italy where he formed another shipping company in 1938, adopting the name 'SITMAR', now redundant following the Italian Government's rationalisation of its' passenger liner services. The

Second World War brought about moves to Switzerland, USA and Argentina and involvement in more shipping ventures, including tanker operation and, more significantly, the acquisition of ex-US wartime standard-built cargo liners which were converted to move displaced persons to Australia on behalf of the International Refugee Organisation.

This activity was eventually to lead what was now the V Group into full-blooded passenger and cruise ship operation alongside cargo ship and oil tanker management. Silver Line was acquired in 1975 and, in 1984, a de-merger from the parent group resulted in the formation of V-Ships which, now based in Monaco, has become a market

leader in international ship management, although control is no longer in the hands of the Vlasov family.

Lodestone was transferred in 1958 from Alva to the ownership of the Alvada Shipping Co. Ltd. of London, another part of the Vlasov Group, and was broken up at Osaka where work began in April 1963. *[Roy Fenton collection]*

SUVA

Sir Walter Randolph Carpenter was born in Singapore in 1877 of Anglo-American parentage and became known as one of Australia's most influential entrepreneurs, businessmen and, later in life, philanthropists. This was as a result of his involvement in the South Sea Islands and New Guinea at the end of the nineteenth and early twentieth centuries, where he established plantations, stores,

trading stations and inter-island shipping services. In the 'thirties he set up airlines in the region and a direct shipping line between Australia, the Western Pacific and European ports, for which purpose, no doubt, *Suva* was built. Launched on the 27th September 1938 as Bartram's yard number 211, she ran trials on the 15th November, sailing straight away for Apia on Upolu Island, Western Samoa carrying a general cargo. Two years

later, on the 26th September 1940, she was back in UK waters suffering damage from a German aircraft off Buchan Ness. Repaired, she survived the war, and in 1948 was transferred to Pacific Shipowners Ltd. of Suva, a company controlled by W. R. Carpenter and Co. Ltd. She was broken up at Hong Kong where she arrived in May 1963. *[Winter's Studio/Roy Fenton collection]*

'New era' tramps

It was 1936 before the first of these 'new era' tramps began to leave the slipways, and it was immediately clear that there must have been some consensus of opinion amongst builders and owners as to what form the new vessels should take. No doubt the eventual decision was influenced by the behind-the-scenes activities of the Admiralty, who were urgently looking for a prototype design to serve as a basis for a standard tramp which could be built by as many yards as possible in the event of war. Their choice eventually was a vessel of around 9,000/10,500 tons deadweight, 425 feet length between perpendiculars and 56 feet beam, and most of the tramp ships completed with Shipping Act assistance were within these parameters, and as can be seen from Parry's photographs of *Eskdene* and *Nailsea Court*, the chosen configuration was quite a contrast to most of what had gone before.

The most significant change in the design of these 'new' tramps was that they were built as 'complete

superstructure/open shelter deck' vessels, rather than as single deck, full scantling with poop, bridge and forecastle erections type. Shelter decks, a progression from shade, spar and awning decks as a means of protecting deck cargo and passengers, had been a feature of ship construction for decades before becoming more substantial structures, leading to some owners choosing to build to the open shelter deck design. However, adequate structural strength was not always provided, and following frequent examples of these decks buckling and failing in bad weather, Lloyd's Register's construction rules were revised in 1909 to control the provision of shelter decks.

A second reason for the regularisation of the shelter deck type of vessel related to the measurements undertaken for gross, net and under deck tonnages, which form the basis for the assessment of port dues and harbour charges. It had long been established that these tonnages should reflect the earning capacity of the ship and, as a result, certain spaces below the upper deck which could be considered as 'open', were legitimately exempt from measurement. Within the original concept of the 'shelter deck', this was deemed to apply to the 'tween deck space between that, and the second deck. Interpretation of what constituted an 'open' space had, eventually, to be settled in a court case.

This led to the introduction of regulations formalising a new shelter deck design, the main features of which were that the watertight bulkheads stopped at the second deck, with the upper or shelter deck above this becoming the strength deck. The space between these two decks was regarded as being open if a small tonnage hatch which did not have a permanent means of closing, and was fitted on a low coaming (approximately six inches high compared with a cargo hatch height of around two feet six inches) at the aft end of the second deck. Transverse bulkheads in the 'tween deck had to be non watertight, achieved by having access openings fitted with a non-permanent means of closure. The second deck now also became the freeboard deck, significantly reducing the draught and hence the deadweight, but the reduction in tonnage resulting from the 'opening' of the 'tween deck brought about the attraction of much lower port and harbour dues.

The change from a full scantling, single deck design to open shelter deck was not immediately evident to the average onlooker, but what must have hit the eye was the outward appearance of these 'new era' tramp ships. Developments in the design of hull form had led to improved fore and aft body lines allowing the introduction of a raked bow usually incorporating a 'soft nose' stem and a cruiser stern. The influences of modernity which were rapidly becoming apparent in virtually every aspect of design - of motor vehicles and aircraft, architecture and domestic life - could be found in the curves of deckhouse fronts and hances, whilst the tall stove pipe funnel, if still required, was enclosed in an outer casing, sometimes elliptical in section and fitted with a cowl top. In addition, the suitability of the shelter deck vessel for chartering to the liner trades was also reflected in the provision of more derricks facilitating union purchase working, and heavy lift gear.

Not all the economies and improvements in efficiency present in the open shelter deck design could be attributed to the work done behind the scenes during the depression by otherwise idle shipbuilders' technical staff and their colleagues at model tank testing establishments and universities. Main engine builders were also playing their part, although their work was possibly made more difficult by having to choose between directing their efforts towards improving the steam engine, or accepting the challenge of developing workable diesel engines.

The main problems with the steam engine derived from the fact that as the pressure of the steam fell, it got wetter and condensed in the cylinders causing loss of efficiency and damage. Various attempts had been made over the years to overcome this situation, ranging from modifying valve arrangements to fitting superheaters, all without a great deal of success. A breakthrough came in 1936, when the North Eastern Marine Engineering Co. Ltd. introduced their 'reheater engine' (described in 'Record 16'), claimed to improve efficiency by 10% over normal superheating. This engine went on to become a leader in the triple-expansion market for many years, and was fitted to all but seven of Bartram's 'new era' tramps.

These seven remaining vessels were powered by a new type of engine designed by Tyneside engineer Albert White. His research had led him to develop a 'compound steam engine' which promised significant improvements in efficiency. Evan Thomas, Radcliffe and E.R. Management were impressed enough by test results to specify this engine for the six vessels they had ordered between them from Bartrams. Greek owner N.G. Nicolaou's *Agios Georios IV* was also fitted with a White engine, as were another five ships built for South Wales company, B. and S. Shipping, later to become the South American Saint Line, by J.L. Thompson and Sons Ltd. Full details of this engine are also given in 'Record' 16.

Postscript

In the event, around fifty 'new era, open shelter deck tramp ships' were built as a result of the British 'Scrap and Build' initiative, with a similar number benefiting from the later Shipping Loan scheme or built from owners' own resources. However, the immediate life of the design was to be relatively short. Within three years of the first examples entering service the Second World War had begun and British ship losses to enemy action rapidly reached devastating proportions, leading to a realisation that allowing tonnage exemption for a 'tween deck which was technically 'open' was not a safe proposition. In addition, the 'open' 'tween deck significantly reduced the vessel's reserve buoyancy in the event of damage. As a result, temporary regulations were quickly introduced which allowed 'tween deck bulkheads to be made watertight and the shelter deck tonnage opening to be closed. As a consequence, all wartime new buildings (including the large numbers of 'Liberty' ships) were completed to a closed shelter deck configuration.

With the war over, owners quickly found they could no longer rely on a 'coal out-grain home' trading pattern and new markets had to be found. Nevertheless, many new post-war tramps initially entered service as 'open' shelter deckers, with owners finding the type well suited for charter to liner operators seeking tonnage as a temporary replacement whilst their own depleted fleets were reformed. On the other hand, there were also owners successfully operating war-built closed shelter deck vessels who were switching to this design for their new buildings. For both types there were other problems in the offing. Naval architects were, at last, overcoming the questions of strength and trim which had generally restricted the size of single deck/raised quarter deck vessels (typically the North East Coast collier) to about 4,000 tons deadweight, enabling the use of these larger vessels in trades such as sugar - formerly carried in bags in shelter deck vessels and now readily loaded in bulk, further depleting the cargo opportunities for the conventional tramp ship.

Eventually the difficulties of successfully managing the problems and anomalies surrounding the tonnage measurement of the 'open shelter deck' ship and its safety at sea led to its demise and replacement by new international regulations which allowed the 'tween deck to be exempt from tonnage measurement even if the watertight bulkheads were carried up to the upper deck, providing the draught of the vessel was limited to what it would have been if the second deck was designated as the freeboard deck, and shown by a 'tonnage mark' on each side of the vessel at midships, adjacent to the load line (Plimsoll) mark. As with the old open shelter deck regulations, the benefit of reduced tonnage measurement also carried the penalty of reduced deadweight.

ALLAN C. GREEN OF MELBOURNE

Ian Farquhar

One of the more notable ship photographers in Australia, Allan C. Green worked in Melbourne from the early 1900s to 1954 and the quality of his material has ensured that many of his images have been used to illustrate books and publications depicting shipping during that great era. He was born in Daylesford, Victoria on 23rd December 1878. As a youngster he went to Western Australia to the goldfields of Coolgardie and Kalgoorlie but came back and settled in Williamstown. He was fascinated by the variety of ships passing Port Phillip and initially developed a keen interest in water colour painting, principally of sailing ships. It was said he had a skill in making the ships come alive and that the quality of his work reflected his great love of ships. Most of the photography around the turn of the century was undertaken by professionals using heavy glass plate cameras. Green established his studio in Williamstown and started to specialize in ship photography. In the early days photographs could only be taken at slow shutter speeds and he really came into his own from the late 1930s onward with action shots of ships under way and with spray. He became well-known and tug masters were happy to have him aboard so that he could secure action shots of ships under way. Regular ship masters who knew him would arrange in advance how he would photograph their ship. He also copied photographs of the earlier Melbourne ship photographers, Charles Rudd (1849-1901), and Charles Nettleton (1854-1900). Green's

collection is all the more important as another well-known Melbourne ship photographer, George Beacroft, lost much of his material in a fire.

Although he made ship photography his business, Green also had a keen interest in ships and purchased prints from ship photographers around the world and sold them in his studio. He also exchanged prints and even made copy plates for a number of shipping friends in Melbourne and other ports in Australia. Former Melbourne tug master Captain Hartley Watson described him as a 'kindly, lovable, humble man who spoke the language of the sea. Cold winds or icy spray meant nothing to him as he made his pictures'.

Around 1940 he donated his collection with an original handwritten index to the State Library of Victoria (usually called the La Trobe Library) but he continued taking photographs almost right up to his death on 25th April 1954. The collection comprises approximately 10,590 shipping images of 4,033 individual ships and includes all types – sailing ships, warships, and cargo and passenger vessels. Most of his paintings he sold but the library has 105 pencil drawings of steam ships and 103 of warships. There are also 114 watercolours of steamers painted between 1896 and 1934.

Some of his photographs of Australian passenger ships are reproduced here. All were single-screw steamers or motor vessels unless stated otherwise in the line giving engine details.

WYANDRA
Alexander Stephen and Sons Ltd., Glasgow, 1902; 4,058gt, 341 feet
T.3-cyl. by Alexander Stephen and Sons Ltd., Glasgow

Passengers: 200 first; 150 second.
Wyandra was employed by the Australasian United Steam Navigation Co. Ltd. on their Melbourne, Sydney and Brisbane service to the Queensland ports of Port Alma, Mackay,

Bowen, Townsville and Cairns – a route commonly called the Trunk Line. After 23 years she was delivered to Japanese ship breakers in Kobe on 9th February 1926.

LEVUKA

Alexander Stephen and Sons Ltd.,
Glasgow, 1910; 6,219gt, 400 feet
Q.8-cyl. by Alexander Stephen and Sons
Ltd., Glasgow driving twin screws
Passengers: 250 first, 200 second.
Also owned by the Australasian United
Steam Navigation Co. Ltd., *Levuka*
was designed for the Australia to Fiji
service, which was reliant solely on the
southbound banana trade to be profitable.
When the Fiji Government applied a
tariff on bananas in 1921, *Levuka* was
withdrawn from Fiji and until her sale
in 1925 ran from the main southern
Australian ports to Queensland. She was
sold to Lloyd Brasileiro, Rio de Janeiro
and renamed *Pedro 11* from 1926 to 1935,
Dom Pedro from 1935 to 1963, and was
broken up at Rio de Janeiro in 1963.

INDARRA

William Denny and Brothers, Dumbarton,
1912; 9,735gt, 451 feet
Q.8-cyl. by Denny and Company,
Dumbarton driving twin screws
Passengers: 150 first, 200 second, 120 third.
Indarra was a luxury vessel with a marble
swimming pool, electric lift, gymnasium
and a verandah café. For the Australasian
United Steam Navigation Co. Ltd. she ran
from Fremantle through to Sydney via
Albany, Adelaide and Melbourne. She
remained on this service until October 1917
when she was requisitioned as a troop ship.
After northern hemisphere trooping she was
not returned to her owners until September
1919. It was decided the cost of refitting
her would be too great and she was initially
chartered to the Orient Line for three round
voyages to Britain before being sold in
August 1920 to Lloyd Royal Belge (Great
Britain) Ltd., London becoming the Belgian-
flagged *Pays de Waes*. She was repossessed
in February 1923 when the Belgian company
defaulted on the purchase payments and
was once more under Australasian United
ownership. In 1923 she was sold to Osaka
Shosen Kaisha of Japan as *Horai Maru*.
During the Second World War she was
sunk by Allied aircraft in position 5.56
south, 106.12 east on 1st March 1942. She
was raised in 1944 but again sunk on 26th
January 1945 while under tow to Japan. She
was again salvaged in 1947, and this time
successfully towed to Japan to be broken up.

ORMISTON

*Alexander Stephen and Sons Ltd., Glasgow,
1922; 5,832gt, 291 feet*
*Two steam turbines by Alexander Stephen
and Sons Ltd., Glasgow geared to a single
screw*
Passengers: 240.

Ormiston was built as *Famaka* for Khedivial
Mail Steam Ship and Graving Dock Co.
Ltd., which she served from 1922 to 1927.
She was under charter to Australian United
Steam Navigation Co. Ltd. for its northern
Queensland service from 1927 to 1936 as
Ormiston. Her owners were Eastern Traders
Ltd. of Hong Kong from 1933 to 1936 and
then Australian United themselves from
1936 to 1955. From 1936 *Ormiston* ran
mainly on the Fremantle to Sydney service
but undertook some Tasmanian tours in the
late 1930s. She had a lucky escape from a
torpedo attack by a Japanese submarine on
12th May 1943 and from February 1944
to July 1946 she was under naval control,
mainly employed trooping. She then
operated on the Melbourne to Cairns service.
She had a major refit in 1951/52 but her age,
unreliability, waterfront industrial trouble
and competition from the fledging airlines
saw her sold to Typaldos Brothers, Piraeus
as *Atlantic* from 1955 and *Atlanticos* from
1956. She arrived at La Specia on 30th
November 1957 for demolition.

WYREEMA

*Alexander Stephen and Sons Ltd., Glasgow,
1908; 6,338gt, 400 feet*
*T.6-cyl. by Alexander Stephen and Sons Ltd.,
Glasgow driving twin screws*
Passengers: 250 first, 200 second.

Built for the Australasian United Steam
Navigation Co. Ltd., *Wyreema* was a
more modern version of *Wyandra* for the
Melbourne through to Cairns service.
During the First World War she had a
relatively brief service as a troop ship from
September 1918 to September 1920. Like
Levuka she was sold to Lloyd Brasileiro,
Rio de Janeiro as *Pedro 1* in 1926, becoming
Dom Pedro 1 in 1935. She was broken up at
Rio de Janeiro in 1958.

DIMBOOLA

Swan Hunter and Wigham Richardson Ltd.,
Newcastle-upon-Tyne, 1912; 3,854gt, 360
feet
Q.4-cyl. by Swan Hunter and Wigham
Richardson Ltd., Newcastle-upon-Tyne
Passengers: 60 first, 90 third.
Melbourne Steamship Co. Ltd. used

Dimboola on its service from Sydney
to Fremantle until 1929 when she was
employed as a relief vessel on the Fremantle
run or on the eastern service through to
Cairns. She also undertook several cruises
from Melbourne to Tasmania, Brisbane
and Sydney – the first cruises attempted in
Australian waters.

She was sold to Ho Hung Steam
Ship Co. (1932) Ltd., Singapore as *Hong
Siang* in 1935 and in 1951 became *Empire
Longford* for the Ministry of Transport
with Williamson and Co. Ltd., Hong Kong
as managers. She was delivered to Dover
Industries for demolition at Dover on 16th
January 1953.

KATOOMBA

Harland and Wolff Ltd., Belfast, 1913;
9,434gt, 450 feet
T.8-cyl. Harland and Wolff Ltd., Belfast
driving twin screws
Passengers: 209 first, 192 second, 156 third.
Built for McIlwraith, McEacharn Ltd.
of Melbourne, *Katoomba* was employed
from Sydney through to Fremantle. In

May 1918 she was requisitioned as a troop
carrier, initially on the Atlantic and later
in the Mediterranean before returning to
her owners in September 1919. She then
resumed the Fremantle service, although
in the 1930s she also made several cruises
to the South Pacific, and from 1937 some
voyages from Sydney to Cairns. She
was again requisitioned as a troop ship

on 8th March 1941 until February 1946
when she was laid up for sale. Sold to
Compania Maritima del Este, Panama
(Goulandris Brothers) in 1946 she was
renamed *Columbia* in 1949. Ownership
was transferred to Neptunia Shipping Co.,
Panama in 1954. She was sold to Japan and
arrived Nagasaki on 29th September 1959
for demolition.

DUNTROON

Swan Hunter and Wigham Richardson Ltd., Newcastle-upon-Tyne, 1935; 10,346gt, 472 feet
12-cyl. 2SCDA oil engine by Swan Hunter and Wigham Richardson Ltd., Newcastle-upon-Tyne
Passengers: 266 first, 102 second.

Owned by Melbourne Steamship Co. Ltd. from 1935 to 60, *Duntroon* was plagued with engine trouble throughout her early life and in the Second World War the Royal Australian Navy rejected her use as an Armed Merchant Cruiser for this reason. On 20th November 1940, while sailing blacked out, she collided with and sank the minesweeper HMAS *Goorangi* with the loss of 24 lives. No blame was attributed to *Duntroon*. On 29th November 1941 she had another collision, this time cutting the destroyer USS *Perkins* in two. She was taken up for trooping in February 1942 and was returned to her owners in April 1946 after transporting 180,000 troops. While under conversion she was chartered by the Royal Australian Navy for a series of voyages and was not returned to her owners until 12th August 1950 following an extensive refit. Interspersed with her regular Sydney to Fremantle runs she undertook several South Pacific cruises from 1957, and from February 1959 she also ran on the east coast from Melbourne through to Cairns. Laid up in March 1959 she was eventually sold to Grosvenor Shipping Co. Ltd., Hong Kong and on 10th July 1960 was towed by the tug *Ajax* from Melbourne to Hong Kong. There she was sold to Kie Hock Shipping (H.K.) Ltd., Hong Kong and in 1961 was renamed *Tong Hoo* for the carriage of pilgrims from Indonesia to Jeddah. She then operated as *Lydia* under the Kei Hock subsidiaries Palembang Shipping Co. S.A. of Panama from 1965 and the Africa Shipping Co. S.A. Panama from 1966. She was sold to Taiwan ship breakers and arrived at Kaohsiung in tow from Singapore on 22th September 1968 for demolition by Hua Eng Copper and Iron Industrial Co.

RIVERINA

Sir James Laing and Sons Ltd., Sunderland, 1905; 4,758gt, 370 feet
T.3-cyl. by Richardsons, Westgarth and Co. Ltd., Hartlepool
Passengers: 150 first, 128 second, 108 steerage.

Huddart Parker Ltd. of Melbourne employed *Riverina* on their Sydney to Fremantle service. Apart from an occasional voyage to New Zealand or Tasmania, she remained on this route until 1920 when she was placed on the Sydney to Hobart route. Disaster struck when she went ashore during a gale on a sandy beach near Cape Howe, 1.5 miles west of Gabo Island on 17th April 1927 whilst on passage from Hobart to Sydney. In the course of being salvaged, she was refloated on 18th August, but on being towed out to sea on 25th September she was swept back ashore and became a total loss.

ZEALANDIA
John Brown and Co. Ltd., Clydebank, 1910;
6,660gt, 410 feet
Q.8-cyl. by John Brown and Co. Ltd.,
Clydebank driving twin screws
Passengers: 196 first, 124 second, 126
steerage.
Following her completion, Huddart, Parker
Ltd. chartered *Zealandia* to the Canadian
Australasian Royal Mail Line (Union
Steam Ship Company of New Zealand

Ltd., managers) from August 1910 to April
1913 for Sydney to Vancouver voyages.
She then took up the Sydney to Fremantle
service for which she had been designed.
From May 1918 she was requisitioned
for conversion to a troop ship, employed
carrying United States troops across the
Atlantic for Europe and then on voyages to
and from Australia before being returned
to owners on 13th December 1919 and
resuming her regular Fremantle service.

When *Riverina* was lost, *Zealandia* was
placed on the Sydney to Hobart service
until June 1928 and thereafter ran again
to Fremantle interspersed with some
Tasmanian trips and cruising. She was
requisitioned for trooping in June 1940 but
was bombed and sunk by Japanese aircraft
at Darwin on 19th February 1942, with
the loss of three lives. She was raised by
Japanese salvors in 1959 and broken up.

NAIRANA
William Denny and Brothers, Dumbarton;
1917; 3,042gt, 316 feet
Four steam turbines by Denny and
Company, Dumbarton geared to twin screws
Passengers: 250 first, 140 second.
Launched in June 1915 and intended as a
fast ferry between Melbourne and Devonport
in Tasmania, *Nairana* was requisitioned

by the Admiralty and commissioned 25th
August 1917 as the seaplane tender HMS
Nairana. In November 1919 she was rebuilt
at the Devonport Naval Dockyard to the
specifications of Huddart, Parker Ltd. and
was eventually delivered to the company on
22nd January 1921. Later that year she was
transferred to Tasmanian Steamers Pty. Ltd.
of Melbourne (a company jointly owned

by Huddart, Parker and the Union Steam
Ship Company of New Zealand). She had
made her first Bass Strait passage on 18th
April 1921 and continued in this service
until 15th February 1948. She was laid up
at Melbourne and after various attempts at
demolition she was broken up between 1952
and 1954.

WESTRALIA
Harland and Wolff Ltd., Glasgow, 1929;
8,108gt, 448 feet
16-cyl. 4SCSA oil engine by Harland and
Wolff Ltd., Glasgow driving twin screws
Passengers: 360 first, 90 third.

Westralia was the first motor ship owned by Huddart, Parker Ltd. of Melbourne and was placed on their Sydney to Fremantle service, extending to Brisbane on occasions. On 2nd November 1939 she was requisitioned for conversion to an Armed Merchant Cruiser, being commissioned on 17th January 1940 as HMAS *Westralia*. In 1943 she underwent conversion to a Landing Ship Infantry and was in this role from 25th June 1943 to 19th September 1946. When refitting for peacetime service she was again requisitioned as a troop ship making nine voyages to Japan followed by further employment by the British Government in the Mediterranean. It was not until 27th March 1951 that her conversion was complete and she made her first peacetime Sydney to Fremantle run on 30th March 1951. From 1956 she also made some trans-Tasman voyages before making her final Fremantle voyage in March 1959. She was then sold to International Shipping and Export Agency Pty. Ltd., Sydney on 15th April 1959 being transferred on 18th May 1959 to Asian and Pacific Shipping Co. Ltd., Suva and renamed *Delfino* for employment as a livestock carrier. She was renamed *Woollambi* in January 1961 but made no ocean voyages under this name. She finally left Sydney for Japan on 19th December 1961 in tow of *Nissho Maru* and was broken up at Hirao by Matsukura Co. Ltd., work commencing in September 1962.

COOMA
Alexander Stephen and Sons Ltd., Glasgow,
1907; 3,839gt, 330 feet
T.3-cyl. by Alexander Stephen and Sons Ltd.,
Glasgow
Passengers: 300 first and third.

Cooma was built for the Melbourne to Cairns service of Howard Smith Ltd., Melbourne, and from 1913 was transferred to Australian Steamships Pty. Ltd., managed by Howard Smith. She suffered a number of minor groundings and incidents in Queensland but on 7th July 1926 she struck North Reef, near Rockhampton, Queensland. Salvors had her floating free on 19th August but within minutes she settled more firmly on the reef and was abandoned. The wreck was further damaged by fire on 26th January 1927.

CANBERRA
Alexander Stephen and Sons Ltd., Glasgow, 1913; 7,710gt, 410 feet
Q.8-cyl. by Alexander Stephen and Sons Ltd., Glasgow driving twin screws
Passengers: 170 first, 180 second, 60 third.
Registered in the ownership of Australian Steamships Pty. Ltd., *Canberra* was twice the size of Howard Smith's *Bombala* and *Cooma*. She initially had a green hull and ran every three weeks from Melbourne through to Cairns. She was requisitioned by the Admiralty in October 1917 and employed as a troop ship being returned to

her owners in May 1920 after an extensive refit. When laid up in January 1925 a fire broke out on board and repairs took almost a year. She did not resume service until May 1926, and now a grey hull replaced the earlier green. From July 1941 *Canberra* was taken up for trooping. Her employment in this role was spasmodic and she was not returned to her owners until August 1946. It was decided a refit would be too costly and she was sold to Chinese buyers based in Singapore. The tug *Rumania* towed her out of Sydney on 5th September 1947, arriving at Singapore

on 27th October. At Singapore she was sold to Compania Maritima del Este S.A., Panama (Goulandris Brothers) without change of name. During her seven years under Goulandris ownership she returned to Australia in 1949 with Italian migrants. She was sold to the Government of the Dominican Republic (F.B. Rexach, manager), Ciudad Trujillo as *Espana* in 1954 and was later placed under the Dominican Republic Navy Department for use as transport. She was broken up in the Dominican Naval Yard during 1959.

MONTORO
Clyde Shipbuilding and Engineering Co. Ltd., Glasgow, 1911, 4,088gt, 361 feet
T.3-cyl. by Clyde Shipbuilding and Engineering Co. Ltd., Glasgow
Passengers: 100 first, 40 second.
When built *Montoro* was the largest vessel in the Burns, Philp fleet. She was intended for

the Melbourne to Singapore route with calls at Sydney, Brisbane, Cairns, Port Moresby, Thursday Island, Darwin, Surabaya and Semarang. In 1926 she was transferred to the New Guinea service calling at Sydney, Brisbane, Townsville, Samarai, Rabaul, Kavieng, Witu and Madang. *Montoro* was placed under Government control after the

outbreak of the Second World War and was not released until June 1948. Throughout her history she had a number of groundings and other incidents but overall she had a very successful 36 years of service. In 1948 she was sold to Wah Shang Steam Ship Co., Shanghai as *Haven*. She was broken up in Japan during 1955

MALABAR

Barclay Curle and Co.Ltd., Whiteinch, 1925; 4,512gt, 351 feet.
8-cyl. 4SCSA oil engine by J.G. Kincaid and Co. Ltd., Greenock
Passengers: 156.

Malabar was the first motor ship for Burns, Philp and Co. Ltd. of Sydney, and she was employed on their Melbourne to Singapore service, but had only a little over five years on this run. While on passage from Melbourne to Sydney in dense fog she struck Miranda Point, Long Bay, just south of Sydney Harbour entrance on 2nd April 1931 and quickly broke up.

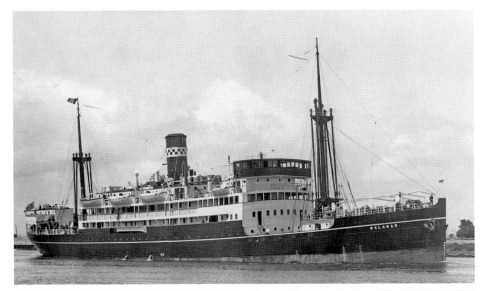

WARILDA

William Beardmore and Co. Ltd., Glasgow, 1912; 7,713gt, 412 feet
Q.8-cyl. by William Beardmore and Co. Ltd., Glasgow driving twin screws
Passengers: 231 first, 120 second, 72 third.

The Adelaide Steamship Co. Ltd. ordered three large passenger-cargo ships for its Sydney-Fremantle service, the first of which was *Warilda*. Occasional voyages were also made from Melbourne to Cairns during the winter. *Warilda* was requisitioned as a troop ship in August 1915. On 11th February 1918 she was hit by a torpedo which did not explode and in March she collided with the French steamer *Petingaudet* (2,530/1897). On 3rd August she was torpedoed and sunk by the German submarine *UC 49* near Southampton while in service as a hospital ship. There were 800 on board including 660 wounded soldiers and 123 lives were lost. She had completed 180 cross-channel sailings from Le Havre to Southampton carrying over 80,000 casualties.

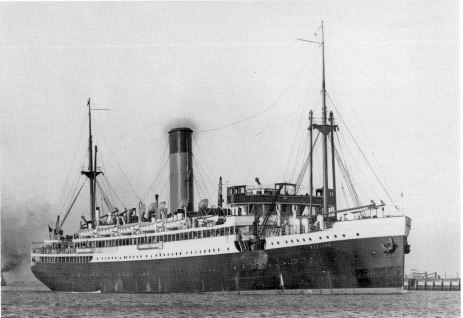

WILLOCHRA

William Beardmore and Co. Ltd., Glasgow, 1913; 7,784gt, 412 feet
Q.8-cyl. by William Beardmore and Co. Ltd., Glasgow driving twin screws
Passengers: 250 first, 120 second, 60 third.

A sister to *Warilda* and *Wandilla*, the *Willochra* was completed at a time when there was a significant drop in the traffic between Sydney and Fremantle. The Adelaide Steamship Co. Ltd. was fortunate to charter the ship to the Union Steam Ship Co. of New Zealand Ltd. of Dunedin. *Willochra* made four trans-Pacific voyages on the San Francisco Royal Mail Service from Sydney, Wellington, Rarotonga, Papeete and return before she was requisitioned on 17th November 1914. Fitted out at Port Chalmers as a troop transport for the New Zealand Government, she was taken by the British Government from April 1918 to October 1919. Still

under charter to the Union Steam Ship Company she was re-delivered to the Adelaide company at Plymouth and was immediately put up for sale. She was purchased by Furness Withy for its subsidiary, the Bermuda and West Indies Steamship Co. Ltd. of Hamilton, Bermuda. She was renamed *Fort Victoria* in 1919 when running from New York to Bermuda. Her sister *Wandilla* was also purchased for the New York to Bermuda service and was renamed *Fort St. George*. As *Fort Victoria* was entering New York harbour near the Ambrose Light in fog on 18th December 1929 she was sunk in collision with the *Algonquin* (5,946/1917).

MANUNDA (above)
William Beardmore and Co. Ltd., Glasgow,
1929; 9.155gt, 448 feet
16-cyl. 4SCSA oil engines by Harland and
Wolff Ltd., Glasgow driving twin screws
Passengers: 210 first, 104 second.
Manunda was the first large motor ship for
Adelaide Steamship, although the company
had previously operated a number of smaller
diesel-driven vessels. She was the last
passenger ship built by William Beardmore.
She was intended for the Sydney to
Fremantle service but during the winter
months was placed on the Melbourne to
Cairns run. From 1935 she largely remained
on this service all year round returning
only to Fremantle when the regular vessels
were taken up for war service. However,
this change was short-lived as *Manunda*
was requisitioned on 25th May 1940 for
conversion to a hospital ship. She was
commissioned on 22nd July 1940. In this
role she was at Darwin when Japanese
aircraft attacked the port on 19th February
1942. *Manunda* suffered collateral damage
and had to travel to Fremantle for repairs
using only one engine. As a hospital ship
she had a white hull with a wide green band
along the hull interspersed with three red
crosses. The funnel was painted yellow with
a large red cross either side. She was seldom
directly attacked. *Manunda* was released
from war service in September 1946 for an
extensive refit. During her war service she
covered 457,777 miles and carried 14,959
patients on 42 voyages. *Manunda* returned
to the Fremantle service in April 1948,
but again undertook Queensland voyages
during the winter. She made her final
coastal voyage in September 1956 and was
sold to Okadagumi Ltd. as *Hakone Maru* in
1956 being broken up in Osaka where work
commenced on 18th June 1957.

MANOORA (below)
Alexander Stephen and Sons Ltd., Glasgow,
1935; 10,856gt, 482 feet
16-cyl. 4SCSA oil engines by J.G. Kincaid
and Co. Ltd., Greenock driving twin screws
Passengers: 250 first, 130 second.
Manoora was the pride of the Adelaide
Steamship fleet when she entered the
Sydney to Fremantle service in May 1935.
She was taken up for war service on 11th
October 1939 for conversion to an Armed
Merchant Cruiser and entered service as
HMAS *Manoora* on 12th December 1939.
On 12th June 1940 she chased the Italian
Romolo (9,780/1926), the latter's crew
scuttling their ship and setting it on fire
some 220 miles south of Nauru. On 2nd
March 1943 *Manoora* was commissioned
as a Landing Ship Infantry. In this role she
was involved in the landings in New Guinea,
the Philippines, Lingayen, Tarakan and
Balikpapan. After the war had ended she
made 24 voyages bringing home Australian
troops. She was finally released from war
service on 6th December 1947 but it was

not until 31st August 1949 that she was
handed back to her owners, having sailed
339,710 miles during her war service. She
returned to the Fremantle run but switched to
Queensland during the winter months. From
1959 she undertook the occasional cruise
to Fiji and New Caledonia. She was the
last of the Australian passenger liners and
had made 220 peacetime passages around
the Australian coast. On 15th August 1961
she was sold to the Indonesian Government
(P.T. Pelayaran Nasional, managers) as
Ambulombo and from 1965 as *Affan Oceana*
(same managers). She was transferred
to P.T. Perusahaan Pelajaran Arafat and
again became *Ambulombo* in 1966. Her
Indonesian owners employed her in the
seasonal Indonesia to Jeddah pilgrim trade
until she was sold to Taiwan ship breakers
on 12th October 1972. In the course of
the tow from Jakarta to Kaohsiung she
developed leaks and sank off Luzon on 18th
November 1972 in position 18.18 north,
120.34 east.

GORDON SHEVES: FRASERBURGH SHIPOWNER
Graeme Somner

Gordon A. Sheves entered ship owning at Fraserburgh in May 1939 just as war clouds were building over Europe – not a very auspicious time to do so. He purchased his first ship, the London-owned *Bullfinch* built some 36 years earlier in 1903, which he renamed *Archmor*. Taken over at Bristol, she was placed in the coastal trade carrying coal from north east England to ports in Scotland. This routine was interrupted in September when war broke out and she came under the direction of the Ministry of Shipping.

Despite wartime conditions, Gordon Sheves expanded his fleet from one to three between July 1942 when he acquired the 43-year old *Plasma* from William Robertson of Glasgow and May 1943 when he added the 43-year-old *Eddie* from Dundee owners. Because of wartime restrictions on the renaming of ships, they retained their original names until November 1945. A fourth ship was acquired in January 1945, the Liverpool-owned *Burrington Combe* built in 1910, and at only 35 years relatively new compared with the other ships in his fleet. All four vessels survived the war, although there were a number of minor incidents. In June 1944 *Plasma* was allocated to convoy EWC1B to carry supplies to Normandy on D-day, but had to be withdrawn at short notice because her engines required repair. She eventually sailed for Normandy some three weeks later. In December 1944 *Eddie* was in distress off Flamborough Head, but made her own way into Bridlington harbour where her cargo of steel was reloaded.

When peace in Europe came in 1945 it was not long before Gordon Sheves renamed his ships more appropriately, *Plasma* becoming *Archella*, *Eddie* becoming *Archallan*, both in November 1945, and *Burrington Combe* becoming *Archvale*. The naming scheme was inspired, if that is the word, by that already carried on Sheves' first acquisition, *Archmor*.

Gordon Sheves' fleet suffered its first major mishap in 1946 when, on 31st March *Archella*, while returning from Kirkwall to Sunderland to load another cargo of coal, was stranded just two miles north of her destination. She refloated some five days later and was towed to the Tyne, where she was declared a constructive total loss. However, a Dundee sand dredging firm bought her to work in the River Tay and she was to give them a further four years of service before going to the breakers.

In August 1946 Gordon Sheves bought as a replacement the *Bronzite*, a second ship from the fleet of William Robertson. Renamed *Archgrove*, she was his largest vessel, and the first and only one fitted with a triple-expansion engine. As it turned out, not only was she to become the oldest vessel (52-years-old) he owned, but also the one that was to give him the longest service (11 years).

With the coastal trade still booming after the war years, fate intervened again in 1948. Having survived the war *Archmor* ran ashore on 11th February on the Northumberland coast while carrying a cargo of coal from Warkworth to Inverness and became a total loss. To replace this loss, a motor lighter was purchased. Like the rest of the fleet *Archglen* was of considerable vintage being some 30 years old and having started life as a dumb barge, British-built but for many years Dutch-owned. Her time with Gordon Sheves was to be short but decidedly hazardous. In February 1949 she was aground for two days near Mablethorpe in Lincolnshire. On 29th October 1949 she was sheltering from a gale in Dover harbour while on a voyage from Blyth to Dartmouth, Devon when she dragged her anchors and was driven on to the mole. Although refloated some 10 days later, she was declared a constructive total loss and broken up.

Archgrove was the only one of Sheves' coasters to have been well photographed. *[Roy Fenton collection]*

By the early 1950s the coastal trade was becoming more competitive with motor vessels replacing increasingly expensive-to-run coal-burning steamers. As a consequence, Gordon Sheves sold two of his three remaining steamers with compound engines, *Archallan* – now 51-years-old – in December 1951 followed by *Archvale* – now 42-years-old – in October 1952, both for further service with Newcastle and Sunderland owners so obviously there was life in them even then.

Archgrove seemed prone to minor collisions, and was involved in no less than three between July 1948 and April 1949, a period of just nine months. She continued to trade until 5th December 1957 when she arrived at Antwerp for breaking up. She had seen 63 years of service under three owners and was one of the last steam coasters in the trade. Her sale for demolition signalled that, after 18 years, Gordon Sheves had left ship owning, having kept in service for that time five old steamers and a motor vessel, of which two were lost, three sold and just one survived to meet the breaker's torch.

The company's major trade had been carrying coal from ports in east Scotland and the north east of England as far south as Goole to the fishing ports of north east Scotland, but the ships made many voyages further south. For instance, they carried bagged cement from the Thames and Medway to Scottish ports, and coal from the Tyne to ports on the south coast and to Jersey. Funnels were black with a red band: no houseflag is known and it is unlikely that, as one of Britain's many small coastal ship owners, Sheves ever had one.

Fleet List

1. ARCHMOR 1939-1948
O.N. 118326 246g 97n
118.7 x 23.2 x 8.8 feet
T. 3-cyl. by George T. Grey, South Shields;
50 NHP, 360 IHP, 9 knots.
13.8.1903: Launched by the Selby Shipbuilding and Engineering Co. Ltd., Selby (Yard No. 67).
9.1903: Completed.
22.9.1903: Registered in the ownership of the General Steam Navigation Co. Ltd., London as BULLFINCH.
30.8.1929: Sold to Lionel F.E. Macmahon, London.
3.9.1929: Sold to Reginald Aylmer (J.W. Harvie, manager), London.
25.9.1929: Renamed ARCHMOR.
12.2.1930: Sold to James and Emanuel Ltd., Cardiff.
13.5.1939: Acquired by Gordon A. Sheves, Fraserburgh.
4.2.1942: Requisitioned by the Admiralty to carry supplies to Scapa Flow, Orkney Islands.
11.2.1948: Stranded north of Seaton Point, Boulmer just north of Alnmouth, Northumberland whilst on a voyage from Warkworth to Inverness with a cargo of coal.
17.2.1948: Salvage attempts abandoned.
11.3.1948: Register closed.

2. PLASMA/ARCHELLA 1942-1946
Iron and steel
O.N. 108792 325g 86n
135.4 x 23.0 x 10.0 feet
C. 2-cyl. by Muir and Houston Ltd., Glasgow; 42 NHP, 320 IHP, 9 knots.
17.12.1898: Launched by Carmichael, MacLean and Co., Greenock (Yard No. 21).
1.1.1899: Completed.
14.2.1899: Registered in the ownership of William Robertson, Glasgow as PLASMA.
31.7.1942: Acquired by Gordon A. Sheves, Fraserburgh.
23.11.1945: Renamed ARCHELLA.
31.3.1946: Stranded between Whitburn and Marsden, two miles north of Sunderland, in fog whilst on a voyage from Kirkwall to Sunderland and beached in the River Wear at Sunderland.

This photograph of the tiny *Archmor* was taken at Truro on 7th July 1932 when she was owned by James and Emanuel Ltd. of Cardiff. She was also photographed at Bristol in the same ownership, but with a 'JE' logo in a disc on what appears to be a larger, replacement funnel. Under her former name *Bullfinch* she was one of the smallest sea-going vessels owned by General Steam. *[Roy Fenton collection]*

Archella seems to have been camera-shy during her short career with Sheves, but this is her as Robertson's *Plasma*. *[Roy Fenton collection]*

3.4.1946: Refloated and arrived
in River Tyne. Later declared a
constructive total loss.
11.6.1946: Sold to Joseph Barlow and
John Sinclair, Dundee.
3.4.1947: Arrived on the Tyne for
repairs.
6.12.1950: Register closed, broken up.

3. EDDIE/ARCHALLAN 1943-1951
O.N. 111299 235g 89n
120.0 x 22.1 x 8.8 feet
C. 2-cyl. by Bow, McLachlan and Co.,
Paisley; 37 NHP, 330 HP, 10 knots.
20.9.1900: Launched by J. McArthur
and Co., Paisley (Yard No. 135).
2.10.1900: Registered in the ownership
of Thomas L. Young and David
Gillespie, Glasgow as FERRUM.
30.4.1906: Transferred to the British
Coasting Steamship Co. Ltd. (Thomas
L. Young and David Gillespie,
managers), Glasgow.
9.11.1911: Sold to the Ferrum
Steamship Co. Ltd. (G.T. Gillie,
manager), Newcastle-upon-Tyne.
13.8.1919: Sold to the Fort Shipping
Co. Ltd. (William H. Thurston,
manager), Cardiff.
16.12.1919: Sold to the Vale of
Glamorgan Shipping Co. Ltd.
(Frederick C. Moon, manager), Cardiff.
7.12.1923: Sold to Mrs Ann B. Monroe
and Miss Helen B. Monroe (Kenneth
R. Monroe, manager), Cardiff and later
Liverpool.
1.1.1931: Transferred to the Eastbrook
Trading Company (Kenneth R. Monroe,
manager), Liverpool.
21.1.1931: Transferred to Monroe
Brothers Ltd., Liverpool.
22.7.1935: Sold to Ferrum Shipping
Ltd. (Thor Hannevig, manager),
Liverpool for £3,500 having been
previously laid-up at Bowling for 18
months.
27.9.1938: Sold to the Liverpool
Derricking and Carrying Co. Ltd.
(Edward E. Knowles, manager),
Liverpool.
8.11.1938: Renamed EDDIE.
24.7.1939: Sold to J. Barlow and Co.
(Joseph Barlow, manager), Dundee.
26.5.1943: Acquired by Gordon A.
Sheves, Fraserburgh.
10.12.1944: Sent out a distress call
in a north west gale off Flamborough
Head, Yorkshire when her cargo of steel
shifted while on passage from Hull to
Middlesbrough. Made her own way
to Bridlington where the cargo was
restowed.
16.11.1945: Renamed ARCHALLAN.
20.11.1951: Sold to the Galleon
Shipping Co. Ltd. (Arthur B. Lowne,
manager), Newcastle-upon-Tyne.
6.4.1953: Demolition commenced by
C.W. Dorkin and Co. at Dunston-on-
Tyne.
25.9.1953: Register closed.

Under *Archallan's* first name, *Ferrum*, her original gross tonnage of 271 and a net of
only 19 meant that she could trade to the Thames without paying dues, and she also
obtained certain concessions at other ports such as Berwick-on-Tweed. However, the
Board of Trade decided that her low net tonnage was a freak and had her remeasured in
October 1913 after which she had an official net tonnage of 89, still low enough to give
some benefit in terms of dues. *Ferrum* is seen in Monroe colours in the Mersey some
time between 1923 and 1935 (above). As *Archallan* she was photographed on the River
Ouse between 1949 and 1951 (below). She has gained a wheelhouse but lost her
mizzen mast, probably during the Second World War. *[J. and M. Clarkson; C.A. Hill]*

4. ARCHVALE 1945-1952
O.N. 129630 448g 176n
168.4 x 25.0 x 12.4 feet
C. 2-cyl. by Muir and Houston Ltd., Glasgow;
71 NHP.
14.12.1909: Launched by Mackie and
Thompson Ltd., Glasgow (Yard No. 385) for
Samuel Kelly, Belfast as BELLAVALE.
1.1910: Completed.
7.1911: Transferred to John Kelly Ltd., Belfast.
5.1913: Sold to Thomas S. Wilson and William
Reid, Belfast.
7.1914: Sold to Henry Burden Junior and Co.
Ltd., Poole.
1.1917: Sold to Frederick T. Eberhardt,
London.
12.1917: Owner's name changed by deed poll
to Frederick T. Everard.

3.1920: Sold to Spillers Steamship Co.
Ltd., Cardiff and subsequently renamed
WHEATVALE.
2.1927: Owners became Spillers Milling and
Associated Industries Ltd.
10.1927: Sold to the Ald Shipping Co.
Ltd., Bristol and subsequently renamed
BURRINGTON COMBE.
1.1939: Sold to David P. Barnett, London.
7.1939: Sold to the Zubi Shipping Co. Ltd.,
London.
5.1940: Sold to S. William Coe and Co. Ltd.
(William J. Ireland, manager), Liverpool.
2.1944: Transferred to H. Harrison (Shipping)
Ltd. (William J. Ireland, manager), Liverpool.
1.1945: Acquired by Gordon A. Sheves,
Fraserburgh and subsequently renamed
ARCHVALE.

10.1952: Sold to the Rose Line Ltd. (Thomas Rose and Co., managers), Sunderland and subsequently renamed DALESIDE.
12.11.1956: Arrived at Dordrecht en route for Hendrik Ido Ambacht where she was broken up by Holland Scheepvaart en Mach. N.V.

5. ARCHGROVE 1946-1957

O.N. 102687 602g 199n
181.0 x 29.1 x 10.6 feet
T. 3-cyl. by Muir and Houston, Glasgow; 108 NHP.
21.4.1894: Launched by Scott and Sons, Bowling (Yard No.104).
5.1894: Completed for William Robertson, Glasgow as CITRINE.
7.1899: Sold to M. Langlands and Sons, Glasgow and renamed PRINCESS THYRA.
27.10.1904: Sold to William Robertson, Glasgow and later renamed BRONZITE.
8.1946: Acquired by Gordon A. Sheves, Fraserburgh and renamed ARCHGROVE.
28.7.1948: In collision off Harwich, Suffolk with Swedish steamer STUREBORG (2,358/1918) while on passage from London to Alloa with a cargo of cement. Continued on voyage but, after discharging her cargo at Alloa, proceeded to Blyth for repair.
28.1.1949: In collision in North Sea with the steamer AFON MORLAIS (965/1944) whilst on passage from Plymouth to the Tyne in ballast but proceeded on her voyage.
23.4.1949: In collision with the steamer BENVENUE (7,846/1948) in the River Thames but suffered only minor damage.
23.12.1957: Arrived at Antwerp for breaking up by Omer Bulens, Hoboken.

6. ARCHGLEN 1948-1949

O.N. 148504 150g 106n
122.3 x 16.4 x 7.3 feet
1936: 3-cyl. 4SCSA oil engine by Motorenwerke Mannheim, Mannheim, Germany.
28.9.1916: Launched by Blyth Shipbuilding and Drydock Co. Ltd., Blyth, having been laid down as a lighter for the War Office.
1918: Sold to W.A. Smit, Rotterdam, Netherlands and named IMMANUEL II.
1935: Renamed IMMANUEL.
1936: Fitted with an oil engine.
5.1939: Sold to Peterborough Shipping Co. Ltd., Peterborough and renamed PETERBOROUGH MERCHANT.
8.2.1946: Ran ashore north of Montrose.
13.2.1946: Attempt to refloat failed.
16.2.1946: Refloated and taken to Montrose to discharge.
1.3.1946: Sailed for Grimsby.
5.1948: Acquired by Gordon A. Sheves, Fraserburgh and subsequently renamed ARCHGLEN.
6.2.1949: Ran ashore north of Mablethorpe, Lincolnshire while on passage from London to the Tees with a cargo of scrap.
8.2.1949: Refloated and towed to Grimsby by HEADMAN (177/1924) for repair.
26.10.1949: Blown on to Castle Jetty, Dover Harbour when her anchor dragged during a voyage from Blyth to Dartmouth with a cargo

Another ship which escaped photography during Sheves' ownership was *Archvale*. She is depicted under her final name *Daleside*. [Roy Fenton collection]

Archgrove began life in 1894 as *Citrine* (middle). Owners William Robertson received a good offer for her in 1899 and sold her, only to be offered – and accept – her back five years later. But the name had been re-used and she became *Bronzite*. Sheves bought her in 1946 and got a further eleven years' life out of the veteran as *Archgrove* (bottom, at Newcastle on 16th July 1957). [Glasgow University Archives DC101 0131; J. and M. Clarkson collection]

of coal. Later slipped off and capsized.
11.11.1949: Refloated and placed on grid.
2.12.1949: Settled as a compromised total loss.

20.12.1949: Placed on breaking up berth at Dover.
6.1.1950: Sold to BISCO and broken up by Dover Industries Ltd.

POLISH LINERS AT WAR

John de S. Winser

At the outbreak of the Second World War in September 1939, there were just nine British troopships: by the end of 1941, to cope with the vastly extended military commitments, this total had increased to 120. Included in this number were vessels flying the Polish flag and it is on the careers of the latter group of six vessels, owned by Gdynia-America Shipping Lines Ltd., that this article concentrates. All six had avoided being caught in their home port when the Germans invaded Poland on 1st September 1939 and consequently all became available for charter by the British Government for military use during the course of the war. Official documents reveal that the Polish authorities were eager to do everything possible to keep their ships in active employment, in contrast to some other Allied governments and ship owners, which were recorded as being anxious to ensure that a substantial proportion of their tonnage was maintained in safe trades, to preserve them for immediate post-war use.

The first of the six Polish ships to be taken on charter, on 11th November 1939, was the North Atlantic service motor vessel *Pilsudski*. Fitted out for a troopship role, her hull retaining its pre-war black but her superstructure painted grey and a four-inch gun fitted aft, she left Newcastle on 18th November. Although her destination had not been officially revealed to the ship's officers, it was apparently general knowledge in Newcastle that she was heading for Australia. Events, however, dictated otherwise. After riding at anchor off the Tyne, the ship proceeded in a south-easterly direction, passing Flamborough Head at 19½ knots at 04:20 on 26th November, until, at 05:35 that day, a mine explosion on her port bow, followed by a second amidships on the same side, caused the vessel to list 10 degrees to port. She was abandoned and, although taken in tow by tugs, sank at 10:10 in position 53.15 north, 0.30 east, a mere 15 days after the commencement of her charter. Nine British and 98 Polish personnel were rescued and landed

at Hartlepool and five British and 68 Poles were taken to Grimsby: all had survived, except for her master who died shortly after being picked up.

The newly-completed sister motor vessels *Chrobry* and *Sobieski* were next to be chartered, on the 22nd and 29th November 1939 respectively. *Sobieski*, on her second round voyage from Gdynia to Buenos Aires, had reached Dakar outward-bound on 30th August and was ordered to remain there and await orders. The orders received at the end of October were to disembark her passengers and discharge her cargo, although it was not until three days after the loss of *Pilsudski* that *Sobieski* was taken up as a troopship by the British Government. She was then instructed to proceed to Lyttleton, New Zealand, where she arrived on 3rd January 1940, at the start of what was to prove a particularly impressive military career. She had been assigned to the first troop convoy for the Middle East and sailed two days later, via Wellington, Fremantle and Colombo. To counter the threat of attack by a German pocket battleship in the Indian Ocean, the battleship *Ramillies* and the cruisers *Leander* and *Canberra* escorted the convoy. All the troopships safely reached Suez: *Sobieski* arrived there on 12th February, then went on to make two round trips between Egypt and the French rail network at Marseilles, before heading for Liverpool, where she berthed on 19th March. In September 1939 *Chrobry* had still to complete her maiden round voyage to South America and in consequence her return destination was switched from Gdynia to London. She then moved to Southampton, from where, armed with one four-inch and one four-pounder gun, she set sail on 12th December for Halifax, Nova Scotia. Already at that port was *Pilsudski*'s sister ship *Batory*, which had arrived from New York on 24th September in order to sail for Le Havre with French recruits and a cargo of copper. The vessel was, however, arrested by her builders and, by the time the situation was resolved by a court decision and payment of US $6,393, she had, on 5th

Pilsudski on trials. *[Newall Dunn collection]*

Right: *Pilsudski* arriving at New York.
[World Ship Society Ltd.]

Middle: *Sobieski.* *[World Ship Society Ltd.]*

Bottom: *Chrobry.* *[Newall Dunn collection]*

Trials view of *Batory*. *[Newall Dunn collection]*

December, been taken on charter by the British Government. Both *Batory* and *Chrobry* were assigned to the second convoy carrying Canadian troops to the UK and left Halifax on 22nd December. The following night, under conditions of poor visibility, the two ships dropped too far astern and lost close contact but were still commended as efficient members of the convoy, which terminated on the Clyde on the 30th. At the end of January 1940 *Chrobry* started one further inbound North Atlantic crossing, carrying Canadian troops and a cargo of flour and wheat, whilst *Batory*'s early 1940 schedule took her to Egypt, Port Sudan and Marseilles.

Norway and France

In April German forces seized five key ports in Norway, in response to which the British Government despatched a Field Force to Norway and, on the 15th, a combined total of 2,435 troops from the Clyde arrived at Namsos aboard *Chrobry* and at Harstad, within the Arctic Circle, in *Batory*. *Chrobry* sailed again from the Clyde to Namsos on 23rd April with 1,429 aboard and, on her third Norwegian voyage, left Leith on 7th May with a further 1,446 troops for Smaaland anchorage, near Harstad. Leaving Hol for Bodo on 14th May, *Chrobry* was maintaining 16 knots on a zig-zag course in Vestfjord, between the Lofoten Islands and the Norwegian mainland, when, 30 miles short of her destination at 23:45, she became the target of German aircraft. Two bombs hit amidships just forward of the funnel: a fierce blaze, with flames 60 feet high, set off explosions of ammunition and four senior Irish Guards' officers were amongst those who lost their lives. With great skill, the master turned his ship beam on to wind to aid the evacuation and limit the spread of fire. Those rescued were landed at Harstad by the escorting destroyer *Wolverine*, which went alongside *Chrobry* and successfully embarked 695 of the 1,017 servicemen and 175 crew, while the sloop *Stork* received on board about 300 who had taken to the Polish ship's lifeboats. Although the blazing ship had been abandoned in position 67.40 north, 13.50 east, she was still afloat so, at 02:57 on the 16th, ten Swordfish and three Skua aircraft flew off *Ark Royal* to attack land targets

and sink *Chrobry*. On the evening of 17th May, *Batory* and *Sobieski* arrived at Harstad with 2,875 troops, six guns and 13 vehicles, with the former ship twice being subjected to air attack the following day, two bombs exploding within 100 yards of her. By late May it had become clear that a British base in Norway could not be held and that all Anglo-French forces would need to be withdrawn. *Batory* and *Sobieski* played their part, leaving on 5th June, the former with 2,261 aboard and the latter carrying 1,762: both reached Greenock in the early morning of the 10th, before continuing to western France three days later to land the French and Polish troops evacuated from Norway.

Many days after the evacuation from Dunkirk had been brought to a successful conclusion on 4th June, a massive operation was under way in an attempt to repatriate the remainder of the British Expeditionary Force from French ports between Cherbourg and the south of the Bay of Biscay. A sizeable fleet of troop transports, cargo vessels and coasters was despatched in an operation which rescued over 139,000 British servicemen, as well as more than 46,000 Poles, French, Czechs and Belgians, between 15th and 25th June. At St Nazaire around 48,000 troops were waiting and, despite a low tide and the danger of magnetic mines and air attack, *Sobieski* successfully took aboard 2,890 personnel at Ocean Lock and sailed for the convoy assembly area at 15:30 on the 16th June. *Batory*, after initially anchoring in St Nazaire Roads, managed to embark around 2,000. That night both ships proceeded in convoy, the latter arriving at Plymouth at 21:45 on the 17th, whilst the former reached Falmouth just over three hours later. It was then reported that thousands of Polish troops were converging on the south-west corner of France and it was resolved that every effort be made to evacuate them to the UK. *Sobieski* was ordered to Le Verdon, then diverted to Bayonne and finally St Jean de Luz, near the Spanish border, from where she and *Batory* between them lifted a total of 9,000 Poles and sailed early on 21st June, with *Sobieski* arriving Plymouth at 10:45 on the 23rd, followed by *Batory* ten hours later. In recognition of their good work, at times achieved under hazardous conditions, the masters of *Batory* and *Sobieski* were both appointed Officers of the Order of the British Empire and the chief engineers of both ships became Members of that same order.

Atlantic islands

Fog, ice and defects were to affect *Sobieski*'s next voyage from Glasgow on 5th July firstly to St John's, then to Quebec. Approaching Newfoundland on the outward passage the ship was forced to stop for ten hours in fog because of the danger of encountering ice, and in both directions her speed was at times reduced to 10 knots by engine defects. She was joined by *Batory* for the return voyage which left Halifax on 23rd July, carrying Canadian troops who reached Glasgow on 1st August. *Sobieski* was then on stand-by for an invasion either of the Portuguese Azores and Cape Verde groups or of the Spanish Canary Islands. Such landings would be necessary in the event of the seizure of the islands by German forces – with the initial troops possibly being transported in battleships such as *Scharnhorst* or *Gneisenau* – or of the loss of the vital Gibraltar base. Either of these developments would result in the essential Cape convoy sailings being diverted several thousand miles via the West Indies. Moves by Germany against the Atlantic Islands would almost certainly follow an agreement with the governments concerned and, in an endeavour to prevent them from giving in to German pressure, much-needed supplies of potatoes, sulphate of copper, coal and coke were maintained by Britain. The internationally sensitive nature of the landings meant that a cover was needed and the one devised was that the expedition was destined for Aden, for operations in the Red Sea area. In order to provide the Royal Marines with additional training in boat work, *Sobieski* sailed from Liverpool on 24th August 1940: she was one of four liners selected to take part in exercises at Scapa Flow. For convenience in the event of the operation being mounted, *Sobieski* was stationed at Freetown on 14 days' notice for four of the winter months of 1940-41 but was released for trooping duty at the end of March 1941 and set out from the Clyde on 26th April for a voyage, via the Cape, to Suez. Whilst sailing between Freetown and Durbanshe encountered such heavy seas that one of her lifeboats was lost and another

sustained damage, as did 19 of her life rafts. At Durban that August her homeward passage was interrupted by the need to fit a new port tail shaft.

Batory set out from Liverpool on 5th August 1940 destined for Bombay, Singapore and Australasia to undertake further troop movements from Wellington and Sydney to Suez, where she arrived on 15th December. During her return voyage to Glasgow, via the Cape, the opportunity was taken to utilise her hold capacity from Mombasa where, during the first few days of 1941, she loaded a commercial cargo of 1,243 tons of maize, 236 tons of sugar and over 200 tons of sisal. Allocated to *Batory* for her 27th February sailing from the Clyde to Halifax were 1,200 RAF personnel, 328 Canadian soldiers and 250 sailors, 100 of whom were Merchant Navy crews. Although the Atlantic Islands' landings never took place, the plans were constantly kept up to date, with a small fleet of troopships held in readiness to move at least 5,000 men. The Polish liner *Pulaski* replaced *Sobieski* on stand-by duty for a time in Spring 1941 and, after her March return, *Batory* was held operationally in the Clyde in preparation for possible landings at Gando Bay in Gran Canaria. Equipped with 15 landing craft, *Batory,* like *Sobieski* the previous year, carried out exercises in Scapa Flow in August 1941, which proved exceedingly valuable in difficult beach, tide and weather conditions. *Batory* remained nominally assigned to the Atlantic Islands' fleet until the middle of 1942 but was released for trooping voyages, one of which involved the onward carriage from Gibraltar to West Africa of servicemen who had left the UK aboard *Llangibby Castle* (11,951/1929). The Union-Castle vessel had been hit right aft by a torpedo from *U 402* on 16th January 1942 and, minus a rudder and steered only by her engines, had been forced to put into Horta in Fayal, until temporary repairs permitted her move to Gibraltar. On 8th April *Batory* commenced the first of two sailings to Canada, prior to a circular voyage from the Clyde, which took her firstly to West Africa, then from Freetown across the Atlantic to New York, before culminating in an August return from Halifax, via Reykjavik in Iceland.

Assault on Madagascar

Between late October 1941 and early January 1942, *Sobieski* completed one round trip to Halifax and two to Reykjavik, then, on 23rd March, left the Clyde for Durban. The ultimate objective was the occupation of the Vichy French island of Madagascar, roughly equidistant between Cape Town and Aden, although, so as not to reveal this destination, the ships were issued with charts of Burmese waters. With the Mediterranean already closed to through shipping and the insecurity of Colombo and Trincomalee in Ceylon causing the Royal Navy's Eastern Fleet to withdraw to Kilindini in Kenya, the risk that the Japanese might use Madagascar as a base, from which submarines or aircraft could attack British convoys in

Sobieski at Freetown on 29th November 1940. *[Ian J. Farquhar collection]*

Pulaski. [Newall Dunn collection]

the Indian Ocean, was too great to be ignored. In the early hours of 5th May 1942, an assault fleet of 34 ships, carrying 14,000 troops, reached northern Madagascar from Durban and men were put ashore at Ambararata and Courrier Bays, fully aware that they might meet fierce resistance. Aided by information about French military dispositions supplied by two locally resident Englishmen, who came out to meet the fleet in their sailing boat, the landings achieved total surprise and the attacking force then moved overland to capture the important naval and air base at Diego Suarez. *Sobieski* carried not only the troops forming the floating reserve but also 24 vehicles, 40 motor cycles and 282 tons of stores but had not been fully converted to an infantry landing ship. Although equipped with 10 personnel landing craft and one vehicle landing craft, her davits were only able to hoist craft in an unloaded state, so lifeboats were left suspended in their falls, for use if required for urgent casualty embarkation. Within 60 hours of the landings, all resistance had been overcome and the operation had been brought to a successful conclusion. The intention was that *Sobieski* would next form part of an assault fleet being assembled for training in amphibious operations against the Japanese in the Andaman Sea and for this purpose she reached Bombay on 21st July. However, the shortage of ships elsewhere resulted in plans being radically changed and on 10th September she was back in the Clyde to be prepared for an alternative operation.

In a previous paragraph, mention was made of *Pulaski*. She was an elderly Polish steamer which had been employed on the South American service until arriving at Dartmouth from Gdynia on 29th August 1939 to await orders. In due course, these orders assigned her to regular voyages between Marseilles and Piraeus from October to December 1939, prior to the ship being taken on time charter by the French Mission on 12th February 1940. Her new commitments involved three voyages from Marseilles, via Algiers, to Dakar, Freetown and Konakry in West Africa, the last concluding on 9th July in Freetown, where she remained

until being chartered by the British Government on 14th August. Arriving at Liverpool on 6th September, she then moved to the Clyde to be fitted out for trooping duty and her first assignment was the 1941 Atlantic Islands' operation, previously referred to, for which she was held at 96 hours' notice. This was the prelude to three round voyages between the Clyde and Reykjavik from 7th May to 13th June. Also at Dartmouth in the early days of the war was *Pulaski*'s near sister ship *Kosciuszko*, which was moved to Plymouth early in November 1939 to become the Polish Navy depot ship *Gdynia*, accommodating 400 personnel awaiting transfer to Polish destroyers. However, by October 1940 the shortage of troopships dictated that any suitable vessel would be pressed into service and, after shore barracks had been made available for the Polish sailors, *Kosciuszko* was chartered by the British Government on 7th July 1941 and sent to Liverpool where her fitting out for trooping duty took the best part of two and half months. Her first voyage from the Mersey on 23rd September was plagued by the need for repairs to her port main engine: these delayed her for two weeks at Freetown, whilst temporary work was undertaken; another six days at Durban for further attention and a month at Port Elizabeth for permanent repairs.

North African landings

The UK return of *Sobieski* in September 1942 was to enable her to be fitted out as an infantry landing ship, in readiness for joining *Batory* and other similarly converted liners carrying a total of more than 60,000 troops in one convoy from the Clyde to assault Vichy French North Africa: 1,500 of these would be transported in *Sobieski* and 1,575 in *Batory*. It was the first joint Anglo-American assault operation of the war and was decided upon because a cross-Channel invasion of France would have been impossible to mount at that stage. The objective was to coordinate a military advance overland eastwards towards Tunisia with a westward thrust by the British Eighth Army from Egypt,

A busy day in an unidentified port. *Kosciuszko* is nearest to the camera, in the company of Cunard's *Carinthia* (20,277/1925) in cruising livery, Swedish-America's German-built *Kungsholm* (20,067/1928) and a representative of P&O's three-funneled Straths of the early 1930s. *[Newall Dunn collection]*

to clear German and Italian forces out of North Africa altogether. The landing operation involved three task forces, two sailing from the Clyde on 26th October 1942, destined for Algeria, and the third, the Western Task Force, leaving the USA one day earlier and sailing direct to the Atlantic coast of Morocco, with its sights set on the capture of Casablanca. *Batory* formed part of the Centre Task Force which reached Oran X beachhead in the early hours of 8th November: by 18:00 that day she had landed all her troops and completed the discharge of their stores and vehicles. The ship had been equipped with one vehicle landing craft and 14 personnel landing craft, one of which caught fire and had to be abandoned. As part of the Eastern Task Force, *Sobieski* was directed to Algiers B beachhead, to the west of the city. The objective of her US combat team was to help secure the town, harbour and airport facilities: during the operation she lost her only vehicle landing craft but all 10 personnel craft survived intact. The invasion fleet had achieved total surprise until the ships entered the Mediterranean but some fine ships were subsequently lost to enemy attack. Both *Sobieski* and *Batory* survived unharmed, not only as part of the assault fleet but also during subsequent round voyages from the Clyde to Algiers, two in the case of the former vessel and three in the case of the latter.

Between June 1940 and August 1943, when the Mediterranean was reopened to through convoys, over 1,150,000 service personnel were conveyed via the Cape to the Middle East and beyond.

One such sailing from the Clyde on 28th June 1941 was carried out by *Pulaski*, which disembarked her troops at Suez on 24th August and was then based in the Indian Ocean area for the next two and half years. She was, however, taken out of service at East London for 72 days from mid-April 1942 for boiler and engine repairs and for the provision of additional accommodation. Her Durban call that August proved doubly unfortunate. First of all, fire broke out in a reserve coal bunker, gaining access to which necessitated the cutting of holes in her 'tween deck and the transfer of 270 tons into her main bunker. The second event, resulting from a short circuit, caused her wheelhouse to be completely gutted by fire: temporary repairs enabled the ship to continue in service, while a new structure was built for erection during the ship's next visit. The combination of these difficulties and normal turn-round activities resulted in the ship being in port for one third of that year. *Kosciuszko* also experienced difficulties during one of her 1942 assignments. Eight

Batory. [National Maritime Museum P21570]

28

Kosciuszko in peacetime. *[David Whiteside collection]*

days after her 13th April departure from Fremantle, on the return leg of a round voyage from Bombay to Adelaide, she encountered such rough conditions that severe leaks became apparent in her accommodation, deck house and firemen's quarters. In addition, to reach Bombay from Colombo, her master was advised to use only her starboard engines except in an emergency, because of wear on her port shaft. In keeping with the other Polish vessels, British nationals also formed part of the ship's company and, at Bombay, the opportunity was taken to adapt the ship to accommodate Indian crew members. The ship's subsequent 12 months' sailings were confined to the Red Sea, Indian Ocean and Persian Gulf and, at Basra, on 30th March 1943, she found herself aground for 12 hours, before refloating under her own power. Her services were soon afterwards required elsewhere and, on 1st June, she left Bombay for Egypt.

Italian campaign
Following the success of the North African campaign, during the course of which 400,000 men had been transported from the UK, the Allies agreed that Sicily would be the next objective, its capture removing the menace of island-based enemy air attacks on Allied shipping, as well as providing a base from which to conduct future operations against mainland Italy. A combined Anglo-American fleet of some 2,500 ships and landing craft loaded in the USA, in the UK, in North Africa, in Malta and in the Middle East, with the British Eastern Task Force assigned the landing area around Syracuse, in the south east of the island. *Sobieski* was one of the ships detailed to carry troops from Egypt and, so as to be in position in good time, left the Clyde on 16th March 1943 to reach Suez, via the Cape, on 6th May. Carrying 12 landing craft, she embarked 1,369 troops – 315 less than her capacity – transited the Suez Canal and left Port Said on 5th July in the first fast assault convoy from the Middle East, consisting of 18 infantry landing ships of various sizes, to put her men ashore at Acid North beachhead on the 10th.

Kosciuszko was a member of the first fast follow-up convoy from Egypt: as a personnel ship, rather than a landing ship, she embarked her troops at Suez, anchored at Alexandria because of congestion at Port Said, and then set out for Sicily on 9th July, reaching Syracuse at 09:45 four days later and sailing for Malta at 18:00 that same day. Some 66,000 troops were transported to Sicily from the UK and, with a carrying capacity of 1,663, *Batory* formed part of this assault fleet: fitted with 14 landing craft she sailed out of the Clyde on 28th June. Arrival at Sicily's Bark West beachhead on 10th July was coordinated with the fleets from elsewhere, after which *Batory* was ordered to Alexandria and, whilst proceeding there in convoy on 13th July, collided with the Dutch *Christiaan Huygens* (16,287/1928) at 04:32 in position 32.49 north, 20.35 east. Both ships sustained damage, that to *Batory* being severe but above the waterline, mainly around her starboard hawse pipe. One lifeboat, one set of davits and *Batory*'s superstructure were also affected, so temporary repairs were made at Alexandria and permanent work put in hand at Bombay from mid-August.

The Sicilian operation had demonstrated that the Italian Army had little desire to fight and losses of landing craft had been much lower than anticipated. So plans were speedily completed for the invasion of mainland Italy, the initial thrust being across the narrow Strait of Messina to Reggio di Calabria, using landing craft and tank landing ships. This was followed by major landings at Salerno, which had good beaches and was within range of Allied fighters from Sicily: its objective was the capture of the vital port of Naples. The invasion was timed for the morning of 9th September 1943, on the eve of which came the announcement of Italy's surrender. The sense of relief felt by those in the assault fleet was short-lived because Salerno was strongly defended by the German army, which implemented such a rapid built up of its forces that the Allied operation only succeeded by a narrow margin. *Sobieski*, which formed part of this assault fleet, had embarked her

Sobieski. [Imperial War Museum, FL12635]

was then under consideration to serve Odessa for the carriage of displaced Russian civilians but *Empire Pride* (9,248/1941) was assigned to undertake that task, which in the event *Sobieski* would have been unable to fulfil. Her 25th outward Channel crossing had to be aborted in thick fog at 00:30 on 13th April 1945, when the ship was rammed in the stern by the British ex-French *Espérance* (5,072/1923) in the vicinity of the Nab Tower. Severe damage from just below the waterline upwards for 20 feet and forwards for 30 feet necessitated *Sobieski*'s immediate return to Southampton for temporary repairs, as a prelude to permanent work on the Tyne. By the time these repairs were complete in May, Germany had surrendered and resources were being switched to the ongoing war against Japan.

troops at Tripoli and sailed from there three days prior to the landings. Naples was captured after 21 days, by which time *Sobieski* was on her way to Bombay to join *Batory* in preparing for amphibious operations against the Japanese at Aykab or Ramree in Burma. Once again, plans were changed and, in order to preserve the fleet being prepared for the Normandy landings in summer 1944, it was necessary to recall infantry landing ships from India to the Mediterranean. Accordingly, *Sobieski* arrived in Naples Bay on 12th January 1944 and left Pozzuoli on the 21st to put men ashore at Anzio P beachhead the following day, in the unfulfilled hope of cutting the enemy's supply lines and speedily reaching Rome. Thereafter until July the ship was engaged in ferrying troops between North African and Italian ports, as was *Batory*, which reached Port Said from Bombay just prior to the Anzio operation. At Bombay, on 14th April, *Pulaski* was fortunate in sustaining only minor damage when the ammunition ship *Fort Stikine* (7,142/1942) blew up, causing the destruction of 11 other ships.

Following the invasion of Sicily, *Kosciuszko* remained in the Mediterranean until January 1944 when she moved to Durban for general overhaul and for the replacement of 1,000 boiler tubes, work which detained her until 25th May. Her first assignment after that was to carry prisoners of war to Kilindini, with the voyage guards being provided by the South African Defence Force. Two months after the Normandy landings in June 1944, an invasion was mounted in the South of France by US and Free French troops over a 30-mile front centred on St Tropez. Over 380 British-controlled ships were involved, including both *Batory* and *Sobieski* which were allocated to the follow-up fleet from Taranto, the former carrying 1,638 troops to Delta beachhead and the latter 1,795 to Alpha. They reached their destinations on 16th August, the day after the main assault had gone in. In September, both ships ceased to be classified as infantry landing ships and sailed for the Clyde, *Sobieski* arriving there in mid-September and *Batory* at the end of October. *Batory* commenced a three-month round voyage from the Clyde to Bombay and Mombasa on 16th December and, nine days later, *Sobieski* started overnight sailings between Southampton and Le Havre for US Army personnel. She

Far eastern operations

Rangoon was the first major amphibious objective for British forces against the Japanese in Burma and the assault date was 2nd May 1945. Elephant Island, at the entrance to the Rangoon River, was expected to be defended by coastal guns but, when no opposition was encountered, the invading force ventured 30 miles up river to the capital which was found also to be undefended. *Pulaski* formed part of the build-up fleet, leaving Madras on 8th May and reaching Akyab, some 250 miles west of Rangoon, three days later. This was the start of a short series of round voyages on that route, the duration of which became extended on 9th July by the ship berthing in Rangoon for the first time. The following month she was detached to form part of a vast invasion fleet destined for Malaya. The first landings were to take place in the Sepang area and Morib beaches, 28 miles south east of Port Swettenham, on 9th September, with the second phase being scheduled for three days later, 40 miles further south, near Port Dickson. *Pulaski* was assigned to the first phase and left Madras on 31st August, while *Sobieski*, which had reached Bombay on 28th July and now had a capacity of 734 British and 1,200 Indian troops, sailed as part of the build-up fleet on 9th September. The operational arrangements were too far advanced for major changes so, even though the official instrument of Japanese surrender had already been signed, the landings still took place but without the crippling losses feared, particularly from Japanese suicide boats and aircraft. Events would have been very different had the dropping of the atomic bombs on Japan not brought the Second World War to an early conclusion. Preliminary plans had already been laid for a US assault on the south island of Japan, to establish a strong base from which to intensify the effort to achieve the unconditional surrender of the Japanese. Fifty of the 120 long-range troopships under British control were to form part of the fleet to be amassed against Japan and these included *Batory*, *Sobieski*, *Kosciuszko* and *Pulaski*, with the last two being approved for use in the operational areas.

Sobieski. [National Maritime Museum, N37409]

With the ending of hostilities, ships could sail into Singapore unopposed, rather than waiting for its planned overland liberation by the Army: *Pulaski* arrived at the port on 14th September, followed by *Sobieski* ten days later. There were around 1,900 Allied prisoners-of-war and civilian internees in the Malayan Peninsula and 17,000 in Singapore and the major challenge was to provide suitable shipping with the minimum of delay, whilst at the same time catering for the substantial movements of serving personnel. Accordingly, the 1,323-capacity *Pulaski* left Singapore for Calcutta and thereafter remained in Eastern waters, while *Sobieski*'s voyage, reaching Liverpool on 23rd October, proved to be her penultimate Far Eastern sailing. Meanwhile, in July 1945, *Batory*, at Gareloch on the 13th, and *Kosciuszko*, at Cape Town on the 28th, had been switched from the Polish to the British flag. The latter ship was to remain mainly east of Suez, whilst *Batory* left the Clyde on 2nd August to serve in the Mediterranean until late December, mainly providing a sea connection between Egypt and Toulon, from where rail services were used to convey service personnel to England via the Channel ports of Dieppe and Calais. In January 1946, the Polish government requested the return of *Batory* and *Sobieski* but were willing to dispose of the two old ships, both of which

were taken over by the British Government. *Batory* was redelivered at Glasgow on 11th April 1946 but *Sobieski* continued in British service until arrival in London on 5th October and was redelivered at Gdansk on 6th November. *Pulaski* arrived at Calcutta on 3rd April 1946 for a major refit, which was seriously prolonged by labour shortages and riots. Renamed *Empire Penryn* on 7th December, she resumed sailings between India and Burma at the end of February 1947 but these lasted only until mid-May. After refrigeration and boiler repairs, she left Madras for the UK on 26th June; was immobilised for a month at Suez by a breakdown of her refrigeration plant and arrived at Liverpool on 7th September. Such was her condition that she was even rejected for service as a Syrian pilgrim carrier in October the following year. On 29th June 1946 *Kosciuszko* was renamed *Empire Helford* and, after overhaul at Calcutta, served in the Far East; in northern Europe and finally in the Mediterranean and Red Sea, before reaching Liverpool from East Africa on 18th January 1949. Despite her 34 years, she was then considered for purchase by South American interests but, in fact, both ships had reached the end of their careers, with their registry being closed in February 1949 and November 1950 respectively.

Details of ships				
Ship	**Completed**	**Builder**	**gt**	**feet**
Batory	1936	Cantieri Riuniti dell'Adriatico, Malfalcone, Italy	14,287	526
Chrobry	1939	Nakskov Skibsvaerft A/S, Nakskov, Denmark	11,442	506
Kosciuszko/Empire Helford	1915	Barclay, Curle and Co. Ltd., Glasgow	6,852	440
Pilsudski	1935	Cantieri Riuniti dell'Adriatico, Malfalcone, Italy	14,294	526
Pulaski/Empire Penryn	1912	Barclay, Curle and Co. Ltd., Glasgow	6,345	425
Sobieski	1939	Swan, Hunter and Wigham Richardson Ltd., Newcastle-upon-Tyne.	11,030	493

Kosciuszko as *Empire Helford* on the landing stage at Liverpool on 28th August 1947 (above). Astern of her is the troopship *Empress of Australia* (21,860/1913) completed as the *Tirpitz* for the Hamburg-Amerika Line. Renamed *Empress of China* in 1921 she was given the name *Empress of Australia* in 1922 following a major refit on the Clyde. *Empire Helford* is seen again awaiting breaking up at Blyth on 16th June 1950 (right). *[J. and M. Clarkson; Roy Fenton collection]* *Empire Penryn*, the former *Pulaski*, under the coal tips in Prince of Wales Dock, Swansea in 1948 (bottom). *[National Maritime Museum P54115]*

Batory (right and middle) went back to Poland in 1946. She served as a passenger ship until 1969 when she was converted to a floating hotel at Gdynia. Her end came in 1971 when she was broken up at Hong Kong, arriving there on 11th May of that year. *[Russell Priest]*

The *Sobrieski* went to the Russians in 1950 and was renamed *Gruzia* (bottom). She lasted until 1975 when she arrived at La Spezia, Italy on the 14th April 1975 for breaking up. *[Newall Dunn collection]*

THE BRUNSHAUSEN REEFERS: Part 2
Tony Breach

Brunskamp arriving at Barry on 6th June 1976 whilst on charter to Geest Line. *[John Wiltshire/Nigel Jones collection]*

Modified ship built for Harald Schuldt

Although built for a different owner, this vessel was of the same nominal dimensions as the *Brunshausen* class. The major differences were that there was no passenger accommodation which resulted in a slightly shorter accommodation block on the bridge deck, the crew was reduced to 38, and the large funnel favoured by the Schuldt company was fitted. The ship did eventually pass into the Bruns fleet indicating that Bruns may well have had some involvement with her from the beginning.

AUGUSTENBURG

IMO 6523169 4,697g, 2,508n, 4,163d.
135.97 x 124.01 x 16.82 x 11.36 metres.
Refrigerated capacity: 285,273 cubic feet.
M.A.N. K8Z70/120D type 2SCSA oil engine
by Howaldtswerke A.G., Hamburg, West
Germany; 9,600 BHP, 21 knots.
11.9.1965: Launched by Howaldtswerke
A.G., Hamburg (Yard No. 974) for
Partenreederei m.s. 'Augustenburg'
(Harald Schuldt (K.-R.)), Hamburg as
AUGUSTENBURG.
13.12.1965: Completed.
1972: Sold to Partenreederei m.s. 'Blexen'
(Scipio & Co.), Bremen, Germany and
renamed BLEXEN.
1975: Sold to Partenreederei m.s.
'Brunskamp' (W. Bruns & Co. (K.-R.)),
Hamburg and renamed BRUNSKAMP.
1978: Transferred to Intercontinental
Transportation Services Ltd., Monrovia,
Liberia (Irgens Larsen, Oslo, Norway,
manager) and renamed TROPICAL MOON
on the sale of the Bruns company to the
Standard Fruit Company (Castle and Cooke

Inc., Honolulu, U.S.A.).
1986: Transferred to Compania Agmaresa
S.A., Guayaquil, Ecuador (a Standard Fruit
subsidiary) and renamed RIO VINCES.
1987: Ownership reverted to Intercontinental
Transportation Services Ltd., Monrovia
and name to TROPICAL MOON under the
Panama flag.
6.5.1993: Arrived at Alang.
8.5.1993: Beached for demolition.

Ships completed at Emden as fish carriers for the Soviet Union

VETER

IMO 6412358 4,716g, 2,660n, 5,218d.
135.21 x 124.01 x 16.81 x 11.36 metres.

Refrigerated capacity: 288,593 cubic feet.
M.A.N. K8Z70/120D type 2SCSA oil engine
by Maschinenfabrik Augsburg-Nuernburg
A.G., Augsburg, West Germany; 9,600 BHP,
21 knots.
Launched by Rheinstahl Nordseewerke,
Emden, West Germany (Yard No. 347) for
USSR Mortransflot as VETER.
1964: Completed and allocated to USSR
Azcherryba, Sevastopol, U.S.S.R.
Owners later became USSR Yugrybtranssbyt,
Sevastopol.
Owners became Yugrybtranssbyt, Sevastopol
and the ship put under the Ukrainian flag
after the break up of the Soviet Union
6.2.1995: Arrived Gadani Beach for
demolition.

Veter at Wellington in December 1979. *[J. and M. Clarkson collection]*

SHKVAL
IMO 6412346 4,716g, 2,660n,
5,218d.
135.21 x 124.01 x 16.81 x 11.36 feet.
Refrigerated capacity: 288,881 cubic feet.
M.A.N. K8Z70/120D type 2SCSA oil engine by Maschinenfabrik Augsburg-Nuernburg A.G, Augsburg, West Germany; 9,600 BHP, 21 knots.
Launched by Rheinstahl Nordseewerke, Emden, West Germany (Yard No. 348) for Mortransflot, U.S.S.R. as SHKVAL.
1964: Completed.
17-18.6.1975: Suffered a serious fire while at Bijela, Yugoslavia. Towed out of port while still burning and beached with the after part submerged and the engine room and superstructure gutted. Declared a total loss, raised and towed to Split for demolition.

TAYFUN
IMO 6412346 4,727g, 2,667n,
5,218d.
136.00 x 124.01 x 16.81 x 11.36 metres.
Refrigerated capacity: 288,593 cubic feet.
M.A.N. K8Z70/120D type 2SCSA oil engine by Maschinenfabrik Augsburg-Nuernburg A.G., Augsburg, West Germany; 9,600 BHP, 21 knots.
Launched by Rheinstahl Nordseewerke, Emden, West Germany (Yard No. 349) for Mortransflot, U.S.S.R. as TAYFUN.
1964: Completed and allocated to USSR Azcherryba, Sevastopol, U.S.S.R. which later became USSR Yugrybtranssbyt.
Owners became Yugrybtranssbyt, Sevastopol and the ship put under the Ukrainian flag after the break up of the Soviet Union
11.6.1995: Arrived at Mumbai for demolition by Chaudhary Steel Alloys Ltd.
29.6.1995: Work commenced.

SHTORM
IMO 6418728 4,727g, 2,667n,
5,218d.
135.90 x 124.14 x 16.79 x 11.36 feet.
Refrigerated capacity: 288,593 cubic feet.
M.A.N. K8Z70/120D type 2SCSA oil engine by Maschinenfabrik Augsburg-Nuernburg A.G., Augsburg, West Germany; 9,600 BHP, 21 knots.
Launched by Rheinstahl Nordseewerke, Emden, West Germany (Yard No. 350) for Mortransflot, U.S.S.R. as SHTORM.
1964: Completed and allocated to USSR Zapryba, Klaipeda, U.S.S.R.
31.5.1987: Demolition commenced at Gadani Beach.

Shkval (*Schkval*) on 11th November 1964. *[Michael Lennon]*

Tayfun (*Taifun*) on 30th August 1965. *[Michael Lennon]*

Shtorm (*Schtorm*) photographed on 15th February 1966. *[Michael Lennon]*

BURYA

IMO 6415269 4,728g, 2,667n, 5,206d.
135.90 x 124.14 x 16.81 x 11.36
metres.
Refrigerated capacity: 288,625 cubic
feet.
M.A.N. K8Z70/120D type 2SCSA oil
engine by Maschinenfabrik Augsburg-
Nuernburg A.G., Augsburg, West
Germany; 9,600 BHP, 21 knots.
Launched by Rheinstahl Nordseewerke,
Emden, West Germany (Yard No. 366)
for Mortransflot, U.S.S.R as BURYA.
1964: Completed and allocated to
USSR Zapryba, Riga, U.S.S.R.
14.1.1988: Arrived Gadani Beach for
demolition.

BRIZ

IMO 6415867 4,728g, 2,667n, 5,211d.
136.00 x 124.14 x 16.81 metres.
Refrigerated capacity: 279,090 cubic
feet.
M.A.N. K8Z70/120D type 2SCSA oil
engine by Maschinenfabrik Augsburg-
Nuernburg A.G., Augsburg, West
Germany; 9,600 BHP, 21 knots.
Launched by Rheinstahl Nordseewerke,
Emden, West Germany (Yard No. 367)
for Mortransflot, U.S.S.R. as BRIZ.
1964: Completed and allocated to
USSR Zapryba, Tallinn, U.S.S.R.
Transferred from Estonia to Klaipeda
Transport Fleet, Klaipeda, Lithuania
and renamed BRIZAS following the
break up of the Soviet Union.
1992: Renamed F.F. BRIZ.
18.2.1993: Arrived at Gadani Beach for
demolition.

Burya (Burja) on 8th April 1966. [Michael Lennon]

Briz (middle and bottom). [FotoFlite incorporating Skyfotos, 102000, 102001]

36

Single-engined variants with increased horsepower, beam and capacity

These two vessels had their beam increased by approximately half a metre to enlarge their refrigerated space. The same engine type fitted to the previous ships of the class was installed but with a higher rating in order to compensate for the extra beam. The passenger accommodation was reduced to six in an owner's suite and two double cabins and the bridge deck superstructure was modified accordingly. Names from the first batch were repeated on these two ships.

BRUNSHAUSEN

IMO 6802204 4,623g 2,619n 5,300d
135.97 x 124.31 x 17.33 x 11.36
Refrigerated capacity: 305,328 cubic feet.
M.A.N. K8Z70/120 type 2SCSA oil engine by Howaldtswerke Hamburg A.G., Hamburg, West Germany; 10,500 BHP, 21 knots.
10.11.1967: Launched by Howaldtswerke Hamburg A.G., Hamburg (Yard No. 999) for Partenreederei m.s. 'Brunshausen' (W. Bruns & Co. (K.-R.)), Hamburg as BRUNSHAUSEN.
1.2.1968: Completed.
1978: Transferred to Intercontinental Transportation Services Ltd., Monrovia, Liberia (Irgens Larsen, Oslo, Norway, manager) and renamed TROPICAL SUN on the sale of the Bruns company to the Standard Fruit Company (Castle and Cooke Inc., Honolulu, U.S.A.).
1984: Owners restyled Mahele Reefer Ltd., Monrovia (Irgens Larsen, Oslo, Norway, manager).
1992: Transferred to Dole Fresh Fruit International Ltd., San Jose, Costa Rica, remaining under the Liberian flag.
29.4.2008: Arrived Alang for demolition.

BRUNSBUTTEL

IMO 6827527 4,623g 2,619n 5,300g
135.97 x 124.31 x 17.33 x 11.36
Refrigerated capacity: 305,294 cubic feet.
M.A.N. K8Z70/120 type 2SCSA oil engine by Howaldtswerke Hamburg A.G., Hamburg, West Germany; 10,500 BHP, 21 knots.
14.9.1968: Launched by Howaldtswerke-Deutsche Werft, Hamburg A.G., Hamburg (Yard No. 1002) for Partenreederei m.s. 'Brunsbuttel' (W. Bruns & Co. (K.-R.)), Hamburg as BRUNSBUTTEL.
19.12.1968: Completed.
1978: Transferred to Intercontinental Transportation Services Ltd., Monrovia, Liberia (Irgens Larsen, Oslo, Norway, manager) and renamed TROPICAL QUEEN on the sale of the Bruns

Brunshausen (above) and later as *Tropical Sun* (below). *[Above: World Ship Society Ltd; below: FotoFlite incorporating Skyfotos, 200933]*

Bunsbuttel at Port Chalmers, New Zealand. *[Roy Fenton collection]*

company to the Standard Fruit Company (Castle and Cooke Inc., Honolulu, U.S.A.).
1984: Owners restyled Mahele Reefer Ltd., Monrovia (Irgens Larsen, Oslo, Norway, manager).
1992: Transferred to Dole Fresh Fruit

International Ltd., San Jose, Costa Rica, remaining under the Liberian flag.
19.3.2003: Arrived at Shanghai for demolition according to one report, but according to another sailed from Kobe for Shanghai for demolition on 16.6.1993.

Variants with increased capacity and two medium speed engines

At the time these two vessels were built, other reefer operators, notably Hamburg Sud and Compagnie Generale Transatlantique, were also building tonnage with this engine arrangement. The twin-engine installation allowed considerable operational flexibility and possible fuel savings, ranging from one engine running at economical speed to two engines on maximum speed, giving speeds between about 12 and 22 knots. In addition, if the engines were fitted with shaft generators they could, while steaming, produce significant electrical power more cheaply than the ships' auxiliary engines and with less mechanical wear and tear. Accommodation was provided in an owners' suite plus single and double cabins.

BRUNSRODE
IMO 6829836 4,749g, 2,702n, 5,384d.
135.97 x 124.31 x 17.33 x 1.36 metres.
Refrigerated capacity: 324,293 cubic feet.
Two Pielstick 12PC2V-400 type 4SCSA turbo-charged medium speed Vee oil engines geared and clutched to a single shaft by Blohm und Voss A.G., Hamburg, West Germany; 12,000 BHP (combined), 22 knots.
10.10.1968: Lauched by Lubecker Flenderwerke A.G., Lubeck, West Germany (Yard No. 572) for Partenreederei m.s. 'Brunsrode' (W. Bruns & Co. (K.-R.)), Hamburg as BRUNSRODE.
13.1.1969: Completed.

Brunsrode (top) was completed in 1969. Following the sale of Willy Bruns to Standard Fruit in 1978 she was given the name *Tropical Sea* (middle). *[FotoFlite incorporating Skyfotos, 275005 and 29495]*

1978: Transferred to Intercontinental Transportation Services Ltd., Monrovia, Liberia (Irgens Larsen, Oslo, Norway, manager) and renamed TROPICAL SEA on the sale of the Bruns company to the Standard Fruit Company (Castle and Cooke Inc., Honolulu, U.S.A.).
1984: Owners restyled Mahele Reefer Ltd., Monrovia (Irgens Larsen, Oslo, Norway, manager).
1988: Sold to Morelia Navigation Co. Ltd., Monrovia (Transcontinental Maritime and Trading S.A., Piraeus, Greece) and renamed

VICTORY REEFER under the Greek flag.
1989: Transferred to Maritime Endeavour S.A., Panama (Transcontinental Maritime and Trading S.A., Piraeus, Greece) and renamed DELOS REEFER.
1990: Sold to Jet Maritime S.A., Panama (Target Marine S.A. (Tony Comninos), Piraeus) and renamed DAVAO TRADER under the Bahamas flag.
17.5.1993: Sailed from Hakata for Hong Kong to be broken up in China.

Brunswick (above) was renamed *Tropical Gold* in 1978. When sold to Monrovian buyers in 1987 she became *Kea Reefer* (below) but only held the name for three years. Sold again in 1990 and renamed *Network Sparrow*, she lasted until 1993 when she was broken up in Korea or China. *[FotoFlite incorporating Skyfotos, 296341 and 79430]*

BRUNSWICK

IMO 6906713 4,749g, 2,677n, 5,475d.
135.21 x 124.31 x 17.33 x 11.36 metres.
Refrigerated capacity: 324,293 cubic feet.
Two Pielstick 12PC2V-400 type 4SCSA
turbo-charged medium speed Vee oil engines
geared and clutched to a single shaft by
Blohm und Voss A.G., Hamburg, West
Germany; 12,000 BHP (combined), 22 knots.
29.11.1968: Launched by Lubecker
Flenderwerke A.G., Lubeck, West Germany
(Yard No. 573) for Partenreederei m.s.
'Brunswick' (W. Bruns & Co. (K.-R.)),
Hamburg as BRUNSWICK.
20.2.1969: Completed.
1978: Transferred to Intercontinental

Transportation Services Ltd., Monrovia,
Liberia (Irgens Larsen, Oslo, Norway,
manager) and renamed TROPICAL GOLD
on the sale of the Bruns company to the
Standard Fruit Company (Castle and Cooke
Inc., Honolulu, U.S.A.).
1984: Owners restyled Mahele Reefer Ltd.,
Monrovia (Irgens Larsen, Oslo, Norway,
manager).
1987: Sold to Monterosa Maritime and
Trading Inc., Monrovia and renamed KEA
REEFER.
1987: Sold to European Express and Trading
S.A. (Transcontinental Maritime and Trading
S.A.), Piraeus, Greece.
1990: Sold to Navex Corporation S.A.,

Panama (Target Marine S.A. (Tony
Comninos), Piraeus) and renamed
NETWORK SPARROW under the Bahamas
flag. NETWORK SPARROW was a
Network Shipping (Fresh Del Monte) name.
30.4.1993: Reported to have sailed from
Masan for Busan for breaking up but also
reported demolished in China during June
1993.

Note on ship lists
In Ships in Focus style, the vessel's flag is
the same as the nationality of the owning
company (not necessarily that of the
manager), unless stated otherwise.

The Lithgow-built *Triona* discharging phosphate at Risdon, Tasmania (above). Completed in 1943 she was the last of the company's ships to have bow sheaves for work on moorings and buoys. *[Russell Priest]*

Triadic (below) was completed at Vancouver in 1945 as the landing craft maintenance ship HMS *Dungeness*. The photographs of her in the Derwent River, Hobart, were taken from the Hobart Bridge. The phosphate cargo can be seen in her holds. *[Both: Russell Priest]*

THE SPECIALISED FLEET OF THE BRITISH PHOSPHATE COMMISSIONERS
Andrew Bell

In that over-romanticised setting of the South Pacific islands there is nothing more starkly ruined than two islands that have been excavated to fertilize the farms of Australia and New Zealand. Ships of the forgotten fleet of the British Phosphate Commissioners (BPC) were specialised from truck to keel, from bow to stern for the phosphate trade. They were required to carry as many as 48 berthed passengers, general cargo one way and bulk phosphate rock on the return: they even had a unique built-in facility for laying and maintaining the deep-water moorings which were essential for their calls at the two islands.

The two tropical atolls, whose terrain was destined to enhance the productivity of Australian wheat fields and the grazing pastures of New Zealand animals, were without sleepy lagoons. Ships loaded offshore, poised under overhanging gantries: shorewards there was a vertical cliff of rock and coral falling away into the ever-restless swell of the Pacific. BPC was a shipping venture that lived with many challenges, not only those of practical operations but also with the complicated politics of its three owners, the governments of Britain, Australia and New Zealand.

Nauru and Ocean Island lie just south of the Equator at 160 degrees east, almost due north of New Zealand. One hundred years on it is useful to recall that, in the early 20th century, both the dominions were, with visions of future greatness, having dreams of island-centred empires burgeoning across the Pacific. They saw themselves eventually taking over from the European colonial powers already established in Oceania. Where Christian missionaries of the Victorian era proselytized, the flag and trade followed.

Foundations

To John T. Arundel (1841-1919) goes the title of being the patriarch of the British phosphate industry in the Pacific. As a 19-year-old shipping clerk in London he voyaged in one of the sailing ships of his employers – Houlder Brothers – by the way of Cape Horn to Peru where, after discharging the outward general, a cargo of guano for the Antipodes was loaded. This voyage developed in Arundel a successful blend of romanticism for the Pacific, a realism of what makes a profitable business and a detailed knowledge of the fertilizers' potential, and overlaid a strong Christian missionary's faith. Leaving Houlder Brothers with their blessing in 1871, he founded the Pacific Islands Company. In good Victorian business mode Arundel established what was to become a vital political link with Lord Stanmore, a prominent Member of the House of Lords. Head office was in London but it was at No. 1½ Macquarie Place, Sydney that was the centre of much action thereafter. It was at this office that a certain George Ellis was puzzled by a rock used as a door stop: it was a souvenir from an extinct volcanic crater on Nauru. Analyzed, it was, to widespread astonishment, found to be 78% phosphate of lime. It thus became the most famous door stop in modern industrial history for it lead to

boom times for two remote, tiny islands and their complex inhabitants in the equatorial western Pacific.

The stone could hardly have been more of a politically complicated portent, for the now forgotten one-time German colonial empire 'owned' Nauru. Nearby Ocean Island was also known to have similar deposits and was only claimed by Britain in 1901: at 2.8 square miles it may hardly have been noticed. Hoisting the Union Flag there was described as Lord Stanmore's triumph 'after much official vacillation bordering on indifference'. The solution to exploiting Nauru was to form an Anglo-German joint enterprise that, despite the two incumbent imperial powers seldom agreeing on anything, prospered until it ended in 1914.

When the chartered *Moonstone* was wrecked on Ocean Island's reef in July 1901 taking 2,270 tons of phosphate rock to the bottom she came close to sinking the Pacific Islands Company too. The extraction of the phosphate deposits started as a pick-and-shovel and wheel barrow enterprise. Sun-dried phosphate was emptied into barges and once again dug out into baskets alongside ships anchored offshore and carried in bulk to ports of discharge in Australia, New Zealand, and Japan. The remorseless Pacific swell, tropical storms and the low level of competence on board the chartered tramp ships resulted in poor cargo outturns, navigational incidents, regular groundings and even total losses.

With Lord Stanmore in London urgently trying to raise more capital with which to develop the islands' facilities, there occurred one of those real life coincidences that can change history. In November 1901 Arundel was travelling across the Pacific from Sydney to San Francisco on the same ship as William Lever, 'The Sunlight Soap King', an ever-restless traveller who had been touring his world-wide holdings. So well did the two men thrive in each other's company that, by the time they sailed through the Golden Gate, Lever had bought the Pacific Islands Company's coconut plantations and invested £25,000 in Arundel's company: it saved the day and was typical of Lever's acumen. By 1903 the company was able to pay a 25% dividend and still meet the ever-pressing needs for development equipment. The results for 1904 were even better.

The company had become the Pacific Phosphate Company in April 1902 and by 1906 a target to mine and export a total of 200,000 tons from both islands had been set for 1907. So too was the idea of a purpose-built ship to carry a share of the islands' exports southbound and supplies of general cargo northbound. The *Ocean Queen*, built to a Norwegian design in a British yard, had a career so short that she never carried a single ton of phosphate, for she went aground on Nauru on her maiden call, sinking back into deep water on the same day. Once again the company had to depend on the uncertainty of spot chartered ships.

Beginnings of BPC

In 1910 there were estimates that Nauru's reserves might be as much as 170 million tons but after a survey in 1937, by when seven million tons had been shipped from Nauru and six million – of a lesser quality – from Ocean Island, the estimates were revised at 80 million for Nauru and 12.5 million for Ocean Island. One problem was maintaining a standard quality. But all this was about to become academic with the changes wreaked by the outbreak of the First World War. The first commercial casualty was the Anglo-German partnership between London and Hamburg which at the time was split respectively 56% British and 44% German. With the German colonies in the Pacific eventually captured by the Allies (who included Japan) shipments were resumed from Nauru but it was the end of the founding company. In its place grew the partnership of three Commonwealth governments, Britain, Australia and New Zealand, and so the British Phosphate Commissioners came into what was a complicated being. It was not a commercial marriage made in heaven. The primary problem was that combining the commercial operations of mining on the islands with civil administration continually ran foul of the differing ambitions of the three governments. It was recorded in the early 1920s that Nauru was run like an Australian country town with all its accompanying amenities.

Although for all but the opening months of the First World War the Pacific was an area outside the main spheres of conflict, capital development of the phosphate islands was stunted. The management, divided between a London board and a Melbourne board, knew what they needed to do, but it was not until mid-1921 that detailed plans were assembled to build a cantilevered gantry out from Nauru's shoreline over the reef so that, poised over a ship, 4,000 tons could be loaded in a day and up to 8,000 tons if loading was arranged in round-the-clock shifts. Thoughts then turned once again to ship owning: the vessel's specification included the ability to lay offshore moorings which were essential to complement the gantry.

The *Nauru Chief* was bought from Norwegian owners in 1921 for £70,000. The maiden voyage into the central Pacific was no less eventful than that of her forerunners. As well as being fuelled by coal, the new ship carried a part cargo of it on her delivery voyage which was found to be on fire on arrival at Ocean Island. On the first northbound voyage from Melbourne and Sydney influenza broke out amongst the crew and passengers to the extent that the ship heaved to and drifted for several days. On the delivery voyage two of the Commissioners' senior Australian employees – one of them the ship's chief engineer – had shipped a large quantity of paint for 'their own account'. The Australian Customs thought that this was the *Nauru Chief's* own stores: there was much trouble when the truth came out.

As so often seemed to happen, troubles unloading the islands' supplies never came singly but two at a time. In February 1926 a chartered ship, the *Ooma* (3991/1905), misjudged the current at Ocean Island, ran onto the reef and was stranded. Within a week another charter, the *Hartfield* (4,661/1915), was hit by a squall at Nauru and dragged the moorings inshore which damaged the lighter jetty. The challenges for both ships' masters can be seen in the fate of the *Ocean Transport* (4,643/1913). She arrived off Ocean Island on 10th January 1928 in westerly weather and managed to disembark passengers and mail but then put out to sea and had to wait for 26 days for the wind to ease, so exposed to the weather were Ocean Island's facilities. On 30th January, at last under the loading gantry, the master kept the main engine running should the weather change and it became necessary to put to sea again: it did change, and leaving the berth the mooring buoy's lines fouled the propeller and within ten minutes the *Ocean Transport* was aground on the reef and, by sunset, a wreck.

This coincided with demand for phosphate in Australia and New Zealand outstripping supply and the result was another torrid period in the history of the Commissioners and their principals – the three governments. This problem was soon to be replaced by one much more serious - the

Nauru Chief, completed in 1921, loading from the cantilevered gantry at Nauru. *[Newall Dunn collection]*

Ooma was wrecked on Sydney Point, Ocean Island on 8th February 1926 on a voyage from Sydney, Australia, to Ocean Island and Nauru with general cargo and coal. *[J. and M. Clarkson collection]*

virtual cessation of Australasian agricultural exports at the onset of the world trade depression in 1930. To compound the problem the BPC had, at last, concluded the purchase of Christmas Island located just south of Java and on a line between Singapore (from where the British colonial administration ran it) and Perth. It was a modest producer of phosphate and an obvious acquisition for the BPC. It was in these circumstances that a new building was ordered from Harland and Wolff.

New ships

The *Triona* was built at Harland and Wolff's Govan yard on the Clyde and the board decided the new form with which to name their ship – 'Tri' for the three governments; 'o' for Ocean Island and 'na' for Nauru. Completed with what could be described as a 'clipper bow': it was shaped thus so that the moorings at the islands could be serviced, or re-laid, the ship's bow being positioned over the buoy being attended to. The *Triona* was steam-propelled and her two boilers could be fuelled by coal or oil, but with a service speed of 10 knots her 17 passengers and 6,000 tons of cargo carried in four hatches took eleven days to make the passage between Nauru and Melbourne. At least the tragedy that linked the *Triona* to her maiden voyage happened before it started. Sir Eric Saltmarsh, recently appointed the London Commissioner and a retired civil servant, was journeying north to Glasgow to see the ship leave for the Pacific when he was killed in a railway accident. Her first call at Nauru in May 1931 coincided with the new cantilever loading gantry coming into service with its ability to pour 500 tons an hour into loading ships. With modifications and a return in 1933 to an increase in demand, the loading rate was increased to over 1,000 tons an hour.

By the close of 1933 440,000 tons annually were going to Australia, 180,000 tons to New Zealand and 45,000 tons to Japan. To ensure stability of freight rates and to have ships where and when they needed them, the BPC needed a larger fleet. Chartered ships were sought by Houlder Brothers on the Baltic Exchange in London or by Elder, Smith and Company in Melbourne. What was to be the BPC's first diesel-engined ship, the *Triaster* was ordered from Lithgows at a contracted price of £206,129 in 1934. As well as being able to carry 8,000 tons of cargo she had accommodation for 40 passengers in 12 cabins and they had the use of a small lounge and a large dining saloon. The officers and crew totalled 62. Provision was made for carrying unberthed passengers in the forward 'tween decks: the number is not recorded. Publicity at the time of the ship's delivery in 1935 reported that the Kincaid-B&W, 3,600 BHP main engine gave a trials speed of 13.8 knots but once in service this was to be 12 knots on 12 tons per day of diesel oil. The *Triaster* was the second unit of the fleet to have facilities to maintain the islands' moorings. The *Nauru Chief*, with a payload capacity of less than half that of the *Triaster*, was sold in 1936 to William Crosby and Company who had close connections with the BPC, being their agents in Western Australia.

Being virtually arms of the three governments, the BPC were aware, even in their comparative geographic remoteness, of the increased international political turbulence of the late 1930s. With their long-established trade links with Japan they may well have gained, in a minor way, intelligence of the thinking in Tokyo. Just how well informed the board in Melbourne was can be seen in their decision in early 1939 to increase production on Nauru and Ocean Island to ensure that there was a six months supply from locally-held buffer stocks in both Australia and New Zealand.

One of the lesser matters considered at a board meeting in Melbourne in February 1936 was to order two additional ships for the fleet. Ahead of the boom for British shipbuilding caused by naval re-armament, the BPC were lucky to place the order with Lithgows, which resulted in the *Trienza* and the *Triadic*. They were a simplified version of

Triaster, completed by Lithgows at Port Glasgow in 1935, had her bow fitted for working on moorings in the islands. *[Russell Priest collection]*

the *Triaster* each with accommodation for only 12 passengers, four hatches in place of five but with almost identical main engines. Possibly the two sister ships were launched successively in December 1937 and March 1938 by twin sisters, the daughters of Sir Arthur Gaye, the Commissioner based in the UK from 1934 until 1946. History does not record if the builders presented their sponsors with identical pieces of jewellery to commemorate the launches.

The chartered Norwegian *Vinni* was sunk on 7th December 1940. *[Russell Priest]*

War in the Pacific

The outbreak of war in September 1939 saw the BPC ships already painted grey overall and the two newest ships each fitted with a gun. The Royal Australian Navy informed the BPC that with the Pacific being declared a danger zone the vessels should keep radio silence unless in distress. However, the first crisis of the war was between the two Dominion governments. The U.K. Government wanted all the fleet to load full cargoes of wheat in Australia for Britain and it took the intervention of the Australian Prime Minister, Robert (later Sir) Menzies, to get this directive cancelled. This enabled the BPC fleet and chartered tramp ships to maintain deliveries in 1939 of 1,200,000 tons of phosphate whilst trying to hold stable freight rates against increasing odds. This was against the besetting problem that charter rates for supplementary ships had, by mid 1940, risen to six times the pre-war level. The diary entry by Nauru's resident doctor's wife that 'we scarcely know that a war is on...' was about to be spectacularly changed.

It had been known since June 1940 that at least one German commerce raider had been in Australian, and then New Zealand, waters. In fact there were two working together plus a supply ship and a tanker. Using the disguises of still-neutral Japanese merchant ships the *Orion* (7,021/1930) and the *Komet* (3,287/1937) had captured and sunk the New Zealand coaster *Holmwood* (546/1911) on 25th November 1940. On the same day the passenger liner *Rangitane* (16,737/1929) had sailed from Auckland full-and-down to her marks with a valuable cargo for Britain of dairy produce, frozen meat, wool and 111 passengers. Despite her vital cargo the *Rangitane* was unescorted and proceeding independently even though HMS *Achilles* was lying in Wellington Harbour. In the early hours of 27th November the *Rangitane* was set upon by the two raiders. One of the reasons for the destruction of the victim was that it had transmitted a distress call. Meanwhile bad weather had caused shipping congestion of Nauru: there lay a concentration of three vital ships and a fourth about to arrive. There appears to have been no intelligence reports given to the BPC about the raiders' current activities. Back on 10th August 1940 the *Triona* who was sailing northbound had avoided the *Orion* in gathering dusk off Brisbane. Suspicious of the ship's identity the faster *Triona* had headed off into a convenient rain squall: her master reported the incident. Within a fortnight of the *Rangitane* sinking, three out of the BPC's fleet of four ships had been sunk together with two chartered ships.

On 6th December the *Triona* was intercepted by the *Orion* when passing north of the Solomon Islands heading for Nauru, and sunk by torpedo. With the passengers and crew taken on board the raider it was described as 'an operation of well-mannered efficiency': no warning signal had been sent out. So lax was the naval intelligence officer that several days later when the *Orion* emerged from a rain squall disguised as the Japanese *Nanyo Maru* he mistook her for the expected to arrive *Triona*. In fact, with 220 miles to go to Nauru, the *Triadic* was sunk as she arrived the next day, 8th December, by the *Komet*. On the same day the *Orion*, having discarded her disguise, sank the *Triaster* within sight of Nauru. Also destroyed by the *Komet* on that day was Union Steamship Company of New Zealand's *Komata* (3,900/1938). The other chartered ship, the Norwegian *Vinni* (5,181/1937), had been sunk five miles off the island the previous evening. It is little short of miraculous that there were only seven fatalities amongst the crew and passengers of the five ships with all the survivors taken onboard the raiders and most of them landed on other islands during the two following weeks. Amongst them were the wives and children of BPC employees on Nauru travelling to the two islands in the Australian holiday season. The effect on BPC's organization of losing three quarters of their fleet within three days was tumultuous. It was made even more so when, on 27th December 1940, the *Komet* returned and, after duly warning the administration ashore to take cover, spectacularly destroyed Nauru's fuel tanks and loading facilities.

With Japan's entry in the war on the Axis side accepted as an inevitability, plans were made in June 1941 to abandon Nauru and Ocean Island and, three days after the attack on Pearl Harbour, a scorched earth policy was put into effect. In mid-January 1942 the *Trienza* escorted by the Free French destroyer *Le Triomphant* evacuated over 1,000 people to Australia ahead of the Japanese occupying both islands with considerable brutality until the end of the war in the Pacific in August 1945.

The BPC had long maintained friendly commercial cooperation with the phosphate mining operations in French Polynesia and upon them they now depended for sourcing any supplies that they could obtain from Makatea, an island in the Taumoto Group 100 miles north of Tahiti. With Christmas Island in the Indian Ocean occupied by the Japanese, by early 1942 supplies from all sources to Australia and New Zealand were falling fast, reaching a figure less than 50% of 1939 imports. To complicate matters the master of the *Trienza* – the only ship left of the BPC fleet – reported that at

The 1938-built *Trienza* was the only member of the pre-war fleet to survive the Second World War. *[Russell Priest]*

every call to load at Makatea it was apparent that there was an undercurrent of anti-British feeling to which the Petainist intrigue added poor quality cargoes and slow loading rates. The British Foreign Office assisted the BPC in re-opening a moribund phosphate mine at Safaga on the Egyptian Red Sea coast from which production of 200,000 tons a year was eventually achieved: it also provided useful back-haul cargo for ships which had delivered war supplies to Port Suez.

With what must have been a touch of the bizarre amidst bomb-damaged London, the underwriters at Lloyds promptly paid up on the loss of the three ships sunk by the German raiders. The Commissioners agreed that the sum should be used to purchase at least one replacement ship. The London-based Commissioner wrote that it would be 'contrary to our particular duty to leave this large sum... lying idle'. The result was the Ministry of War Transport agreeing to allocate a building berth at Lithgows for one Y-type standard, 9,500 deadweight, five-hatch, coal-fired cargo steamer which came into service in 1943 as the *Triona* (2). However, it took over a year's lobbying by the BPC to get control of their ship from the Ministry of Shipping and only then in early 1944 was it on condition that she was used to carry Australian wheat to famine-stricken India and then, at last, load phosphate of dubious quality from Egypt. Hard used were the *Triona*'s new boilers which caused problems by leaking which 'seemed to make her wheeze', but at least she had been built with the facility to lay and service the islands' moorings.

Rebuilding

During the Japanese occupation an airstrip was built on Nauru that became operational in 1943. The island thereafter received almost daily attention from the United States Army Air Force to such an extent that the BPC politely asked the Supreme Commander (Pacific) to restrain his aviators from destroying absolutely everything on the eight square miles that comprised the atoll. Although the Japanese surrendered and were ejected in September 1945, it was almost three

years before exports of phosphate were resumed in 1947 and all the drying and handling equipment restored or replaced. Even then the loading rate was a mere 1,700 tons per day where it had been possible to expect 1,000 tons per hour in 1940. The combined exports of Ocean Island and Nauru were only 200,000 tons in 1948 but had doubled one year later: they eventually peaked at 4.4 million in 1966, a figure that included the output of Christmas Island.

The re-establishment of the production flow was beset with a torrent of new problems, these included the United Nations' moves on de-colonialisation, labour relations problems, the taxation intentions of the British Colonial Office, capital expenditure on Christmas Island's puny facilities and, possibly the biggest of all, the re-settlement of the Ocean Islanders (Banabans) as their 2.8 square mile atoll was being mined away. They were eventually re-settled on Rabi in the Fijian archipelago.

W.R. Carpenter was a Sydney-based company trading in the Pacific which, at the end of the Second World War, needed to replace one ship lost and supplement two others. Their Canadian connections gave them their chance in Vancouver during 1946. To support the expanding British Pacific Fleet, the Royal Navy had, in 1944, placed an order for 21 ships at the three British Columbian shipyards. The ships were basically Canadian 'Fort' types and intended as five different variations of maintenance and repair ships which, had the Pacific war lasted as long as had been expected, would have joined the fleet train. Eleven of the group were delivered to the Royal Navy and the Royal Canadian Navy which left the builders with ten ships paid for, but not wanted by the two navies. Carpenters bought four of them in 1946-1947 in various stages of completion for their original intended purposes. The first to be delivered was HMS *Dungeness* which was completed as the *Levuka*, a name which reflected W.R. Carpenter's extensive interests in Fiji. Utilizing the extensive accommodation already completed, the builders, West Coast Shipbuilders Ltd., delivered the *Levuka* with cabins for 60 passengers. The maiden voyage from Vancouver to Sydney and Melbourne took place in February and March 1948. With her 2,500 IHP reciprocating steam engine producing a service speed of 11 knots the trans-Pacific crossing took 26 days. When the *Levuka* arrived in Melbourne she was almost under the windows of the BPC's head office: they needed ships, and a slow service speed and a high oil fuel consumption of 30 tons per day did not deter them from the chance of a quick purchase. So having arrived in Melbourne as the *Levuka* she sailed in mid-May as the *Triadic* (2). The sister ship *Lakemba* (ex HMS *Spurn Point*) established a regular trans-Pacific service in May 1948 which continued until, on her last scheduled voyage in October 1967, she was wrecked on a Fijian reef, abandoned as unsalvageable and she slid off and sank. Carpenters sold the third and fourth ships to P&O in 1947, the *Lautoka* (7,367/1945) becoming the *Devanha* (2) and the *Rabaul* (2) (7,371/1046) the *Dongola* (2).

Passenger cargo ships

The BPC had hopes that the first of two new ships could be ordered from Australian shipyards, which had been expanded during the Second World War. But the prices quoted were too high so, in July 1951, the order for the *Triaster* (2) was placed with Harland and Wolff. This happy event coincided with a sad one, the death of the New Zealander Sir Arthur Ellis – the last living link with those pioneers of the 1890s. So full were the order books of Harland and Wolff that building the new ship at their Govan yard on the Upper Clyde did not commence until 1953. The ship produced was probably the result of giving Harland and Wolff's naval architects an outline brief of what was wanted and leaving them to shape the design. The result, as it usually had been with this famous company, was an outstanding ship: practical for the purposes of her employment and modern to the last detail. Indeed, her lines and appearance could have her claim

to be one of the finest looking passenger cargo ships of the post-war building boom. She was perhaps not as spectacular as a batch of Port Line cargo ships or as extensively streamlined as a trio that Vickers built for Argentina, but the *Triaster* was strikingly elegant.

In a hull 531 feet in length, with a beam of 67 feet and on a draft of 28 feet, 12,690 tons of cargo could be carried in six holds accessed through six hatches all of which were of the same size of 28 feet by 28 feet, which enabled the holds to be pillarless – unusual for the time. The *Triaster* was also built as a Class 1 Passenger Ship, for 48 passengers could be carried in cabins on the boat and saloon decks. At the forward end of the latter was the lounge and the dining saloon seating 67, and a verandah cafe on the former. The Australian ratings were accommodated in 48 single-berth cabins: only the four cadets shared two cabins. All the accommodation was air conditioned by Hall Thermotank plants. The most out-of-the-ordinary feature that Harland and Wolff had to build in the *Triaster* was the large space under the forecastle head where a special mooring winch was located capable of handling deep moorings needing up to 1,620 feet of 8-inch wire or cable chains. To lay the required moorings the heavily-raked swan bow incorporated a roller in the stem just inside a closable aperture. This system was an uprated arrangement of that developed on the BPC's earlier ships.

The *Triaster*'s main engine was a two-stroke, single-acting, opposed-piston, cross-head, H&W-B&W-type, six-cylinder diesel producing 6,300 BHP at 110 RPM. The ship's service speed was 14 knots. Special filter ventilation systems were designed to keep phosphate dust out of machinery spaces. All the hatches were served by derricks with a safe working load of five tons: these enabled the phosphate to be grab discharged, three tons at a time, at destination ports. At Melbourne northbound general

Triadic was completed at Vancouver in 1945 as the landing craft maintenance ship *Dungeness*. [Russell Priest]

Tri-Ellis was completed at Govan in 1958. *[Russell Priest]*

cargo was loaded into the 'tween decks. There were 5,340 cubic feet of refrigerated cargo space in six lockers between numbers 4 and 5 'tween decks.

Following her near sister ship into service three years later in 1958 was the *Tri-Ellis*. Needing to carry only 12 passengers, the Harland and Wolff Drawing Office at Belfast re-arranged the newer ship's accommodation resulting in it being more spacious. All the passenger cabins with a lounge and verandah were now located and self contained on the boat deck. The deadweight was increased to 13,750 tons on a draught of 30 feet. Experience with the *Triaster* in service resulted in some small changes: the capacity of the ballast water wing tanks in the forward 'tween decks was reduced: these were installed to enhance the ships' sea kindliness when loaded down to her marks as neither had stabilizers. The two new ships' maiden voyages to Nauru and Ocean Island were free of the untoward incidents that had been associated with those of previous BPC ships.

Endgame

Into the 1960s the future political status of Nauru and Ocean Island became a matter of international attention. The tininess of their land areas (respectively eight and two square miles) were in inverse proportion to the attention that their indigenous population sought and international agencies lead by the United Nations Trusteeship Council supplied. The one-time Nauru school teacher Hammer deRobert (1922-1992) demanded independence - which was achieved on 31st January 1968. Ocean Island's future was complicated by the stark fact that the Island had been desolated. All this was concurrent with the United Kingdom Government's de-colonialization of its possessions in the Central Pacific. But the biggest complication was the islanders suing the United

Kingdom in what became five-year-long, twin legal cases demanding Australian $21million and $100 million. As Sir Robert McGarry, who heard the cases, said with some understatement, 'This is litigation on a grand scale'. Early in 1975 with the legal costs having reached A$3 million the cases were settled out of court for figures much less than the Banabans had sought. Independent Nauru rejected almost every facet of a proposed partnership proffered by the BPC. Nauru had always been the main source of phosphate and its carriage had shaped shipping services. The Nauruans succeeded because, to quote the definitive history of the BPC by Williams and Macdonald, 'The partner governments were divided amongst themselves and, moreover, they valued their international reputations more highly than the phosphate'. The BPC, seen as a visible symbol of foreign domination, had no part to play. Their assets on Nauru were bought, eventually, for A$21million in April 1969, a year ahead of schedule. The commercial activity of the BPC lingered on with the operations on Ocean Island divorced from those on Nauru and leading to separation and modernisation of phosphate production on Christmas Island in the Eastern Indian Ocean. Without participation by the UK government, and later New Zealand, it became an all-Australian venture.

Increasingly chartered-in bulk carriers were used by the new Nauru Phosphate Company resulting in the BPC selling the *Triaster* (2) in 1970 and the *Tri-Ellis* in 1974. With a Labor Party government in Australia legislating that ships in the Christmas Island trade all be crewed by Australians, the *Triadic* (2) sale was deferred until 1974. In 1970 the government of Nauru took delivery of the *Eigamoiya* built by Robb-Caledon at Leith. There is more than a touch of the BPC fleet about her and the Commissioners may well have been the initiators of the order. With a deadweight of only 5,862 tons on a draught of

22.5 feet and three main cargo hatches, it was stated at the time of her delivery that with phosphate mining winding down she had been designed to establish a Central Pacific inter-island service. This was not to be, as the *Eigamoiya* is best remembered in Australian ports for the frequency with which she was arrested with her under-capitalised owners unable to meet her operating expenses. On 25th November 1979 the chartered *Cape Hawk* (14,710/1971) loaded the last ever cargo from Ocean Island. Ellis had originally estimated that there was six million tons to be mined: he was wrong by 14 million tons.

The BPC's last involvement in shipping was a ten-year time charter fixed with the Norwegian company Ditlev-Simonsen in 1968. This company had links with the BPC dating back to the 1930s: the *Vinni* sunk by the German raider in 1940 was one of their fleet. The *Valetta* had been built specifically for the BPC's trades as a 27,484 deadweight ton, seven-hatch, geared bulker with accommodation for 12 passengers, a container capacity and even the ability to carry and pump fresh water ashore at Nauru. Used in the Christmas Island trade her charter continued until 1981 when she was sold to Hong Kong owners. By then the BPC and the Christmas Island Phosphate Company had served their purpose in fulfilling their vital role for New Zealand and Australia. As the BPC's historians record 'The demise of these islands' operations was inevitable because they had become symbols of a past age; colonial administrations that had served their purpose but lived beyond their time'.

As a postscript, the profligate spending of an independent Nauru can be appreciated from just two figures: in 1991 their Government's reserves were A$1.3 billion, by 2002 this had been dwindled to A$138 million. During the 1970s and 1980s spending had made them the wealthiest per capita population in the world. There had been the Nauru Shipping Line with a fleet that traded on the flimsiest of commercial hopes and there was even an airline, both squanderously mis-managed, to which was added a catalogue of ruinous investments in everything from speculative property to a Melbourne football club. In 2012 Nauru is dependent on Australian government for financial aid.

The Nauru government-owned, Leith-built *Eigamoiya*. [Russell Priest]

The *Cape Hawke* on charter from Scottish Ship Management (above) and Ditlev-Simonsen's *Valetta*, purpose-built for BPC work (below). [Above: Garry Bain, below: Russell Priest]

Nauru Chief. [Allan C. Green/Russell Priest collection]

Fleet list

1. NAURU CHIEF 1921-1936
O.N. 146565 2,934g 2,047n 3,900d.
289.5 x 44.1 x 26.9 feet.
Complement: 17 passengers, 50 crew.
T.3-cyl. by Nylands Verksted, Oslo, Norway;
225 NHP, 10 knots on 10 tons coal per day.
6.1921. Completed by Nylands Verksted,
Oslo (Yard No. 259) for A.R. Dickinson
(A.H. Gaze, managers) London on behalf
of the British Phosphate Commissioners,
London and Melbourne as NAURU CHIEF.
She was ordered by Thor Thoresen junior
and is believed to have been launched as
NYLAND.

1936. Sold to William Crosby and Co. Pty.
Ltd., Melbourne, Australia.
1936: Sold to Borges Rederi A/S (Hans
Borge), Tønsberg, Norway and renamed
RIO RIMAC.
1936: Renamed WILFORD.
6.6.1942: Shelled and sunk by the Japanese
submarine I-18 off Portugese East Africa
in position 20.27 south, 36.27 east whilst
on a voyage from Mombasa to Lourenço
Marques in ballast. Nine members of the
crew of 46 were lost. Some sources give the
date of loss as 7 or 8.6.1942.

2. TRIONA (1) 1931-1940
O.N. 162559 4,413g 2,590n 6,850d.

401.0 (389.5 b.p.) x 54.1 x 24.5 feet
Complement: 17 passengers, 61 crew.
T. 3-cyl. by J.G. Kincaid and Co. Ltd.,
Greenock; 534 NHP, 11 knots on 20 tons
fuel oil per day.
3.1931. Completed by Harland and Wolff
Ltd., Govan (Yard No. 911) for the British
Phosphate Commissioners, London and
Melbourne as TRIONA.
6.12.1940: Shelled and torpedoed by German
auxiliary cruisers ORION and KOMET
220 miles south of Nauru in position 05.12
south, 165.39 east whilst on a voyage from
Melbourne to Ocean Island. Four members
of the crew of 64 were lost, the remainder
being landed on Emirau Island on 21.12.1940.

Triona (1). [Allan C. Green/Russell Priest collection]

3. TRIASTER (1) 1935-1940
O.N. 163577 6,032g 3,564n 8,150d.
437.6 (423.2 b.p.) x 58.2 x 25.7 feet.
Complement: 40 passengers, 62 crew.
Burmeister & Wain/Kincaid 8-cyl.
4SCSA oil engine by J.G. Kincaid
and Co. Ltd., Greenock; 653 BHP, 12
knots on 12 tons diesel oil per day.
3.1935. Completed by Lithgows Ltd.,
Port Glasgow (Yard No. 872) for
British Phosphate Commissioners,
London and Melbourne as
TRIASTER.
8.12.1940: Captured and sunk with
explosives by the German auxiliary
cruiser ORION, off Nauru in
position 00.54 south, 167.24 east.
Fourteen of the crew of 60 and one
of three passengers were taken as
prisoners-of-war some of whom were
transferred to Germany.

4. TRIENZA 1938-1964
O.N. 166363 6,378g 3,502n 9,656d.
457.7 (442.3b.p.) x 60.0 x 25.0 feet.
Complement: 12 passengers, 61 crew.
Burmeister & Wain/Kincaid 8-cyl.
4SCSA oil engine by J.G. Kincaid
and Co. Ltd., Greenock; 653 BHP, 12
knots on 12 tons diesel oil per day.
2.1938. Completed by Lithgows Ltd.,
Port Glasgow (Yard No. 896) for
British Phosphate Commissioners,
London and Melbourne as TRIENZA.
1964. Sold to Hwa Aun Co. (Hong
Kong) Ltd. (Chip Hwa Shipping and
Trading Co. Ltd.), Hong Kong and
renamed LEE AUN.
27.8.1967: Arrived at Singapore for
breaking up National Iron and Steel
Mills Ltd.

Triaster.   [Allan C. Green/State Library of Victoria]

Pre-war (middle) and post-war (bottom) views of *Trienza* of 1938. *[Alan C. Green/State Library of Victoria; Russell Priest]*

Triadic (1). *[Allan C. Green/State Library of Victoria]*

5. TRIADIC (1) 1938-1940
O.N. 166448 6,378g 5,500n 9650d.
457.5 (442.3 b.p.) x 60.0 x 29.8 feet.
Complement: 12 passengers, 58 crew.
Burmeister & Wain/Kincaid 8-cyl. 4SCSA
oil engine by J.G. Kincaid and Co. Ltd.,
Greenock; 653 BHP, 12 knots on 12 tons
diesel oil per day.
5.1938: Completed by Lithgows Ltd.,
Port Glasgow (Yard No. 909) for British
Phosphate Commissioners, London and
Melbourne as TRIADIC.

8.12.1940: Captured, torpedoed and sunk
with explosives by the German auxiliary
cruiser ORION off Nauru in position
00.43 south, 167.20 east. One member
of the crew of 61 was killed and 11 taken
prisoner. The remainder with the eight
passengers were landed on Emirau Island
on 21.12.1940.

6. TRIONA (2) 1943-1960
O.N. 168387 7,283g 4,020n 9,500d.
462.8 (447.8 b.p) x 56.3 x 34.3 feet.

Complement: 12 passengers, 70 crew.
T.3-cyl. by J.G. Kincaid and Co. Ltd.,
Greenock; 11 knots on 48 tons of coal (as
built).
2.1943: Completed by Lithgows Ltd.,
Port Glasgow (Yard No. 974) for British
Phosphate Commissioners, London and
Melbourne as TRIONA.
2.5.1960: Arrived at Hong Kong to be
broken up by Hong Kong Chiap Hua
Manufactory Co. (1947) Ltd.

Triona (2) arriving at Dunedin during 1957. *[Ian J. Farquhar]*

7. TRIADIC (2) 1948-1977

O.N. 181713 7,461g 5,431n 9,853d.
439.5 (426.8 b.p.) x 57.2 x 34.9 feet
Complement: 38 passengers, 64 crew.
T.3-cyl. by Canadian Allis-Chalmers Ltd.,
Montreal, Canada; 11 knots on 30 tons fuel
oil per day.
10.1945: Completed by West Coast
Shipbuilders Ltd., Vancouver, British
Columbia (Yard No. 152) for the Royal
Navy as the landing craft maintenance ship
HMS DUNGENESS.
1947: Sold to Pacific Shipowners Ltd., Suva,
Fiji, converted to a passenger and dry cargo
vessel and renamed LEVUKA.
5.1948: Acquired by British Phosphate
Commissioners, London and Melbourne and
renamed TRIADIC.
Prior to 6.3.1977: Arrived at Shanghai to be
broken up.

8. TRIASTER (2) 1955-1970

O.N. 186304 9,994g 5,497n 11,993d.
Refrigerated space: 5,340 cubic feet.
531.5 x 67.7 x 28.8 feet
Complement: 48 passengers, 79 crew.
6-cyl. 2SCSA oil engine by Harland and
Wolff Ltd., Govan; 6,500 BHP, 15.5 knots
on 31 tons per day.
10.1955. Completed by Harland and Wolff
Ltd., Govan (Yard No. 1496) for British
Phosphate Commissioners, London and
Melbourne as TRIASTER.
1970. Sold to Nauru Local Government
Council, Nauru and renamed ROSIE D.
1975. Sold to Taiyuan Shipping Inc.,
Monrovia, Liberia (Anglo-Eastern Shipping
Co. Ltd., Hong Kong), and renamed
TAIYUAN under the Somali flag.
1976: Registered in Panama.
3.2.1978: Arrived at Kaohsiung to be broken
up by Chien Nan Steel and Iron Co. Ltd.
8.3.1978: Work began

Triadic (2) (top). *[Allan C. Green/State Library of Victoria]*
Triaster (2) on trials (middle) *[Newall Dunn collection]*
Rosie D, formerly *Triaster (2),* in Otago Harbour. *[Ian J. Farquhar]*

9. TRI-ELLIS 1958-1974

O.N. 300787 11,761g 6,227n 13,950d.
Refrigerated space 1,912 cubic feet.
531.5 x 68.6 x 30.3 feet.
7-cyl. 2SCSA oil engine by Harland and
Wolff Ltd., Govan; 6,500 BHP, 14.5 knots
on 29 tons per day
Complement: 12 passengers, 69 crew.
10.1958. Completed by Harland and Wolff
Ltd., Govan (Yard No. 1581) for British
Phosphate Commissioners, London and
Melbourne as TRI-ELLIS.
1974. Sold to the Nauru Local Government
Council, Nauru and renamed TRYPHENA.
1978: Sold to Man Tat Shipping Ltd.,
Monrovia, Liberia (Hesco Ships
Management Ltd., Hong Kong) and renamed
MAN TAT under the Panama flag.
Prior to 2.9.1980: Arrived at Kaohsiung
1980 to be broken up by Sing Cheng Yung
Iron and Steel Co. Ltd
13.10.1980: Work began.

Managed ship

ISLANDER 1949-1960

O.N. 161325 1,598g 760n 1,912d.
253. 9 (240.0 b.p.) x 41.9 x 14.9 feet
T. 6-cyl. by Plenty and Son Ltd., Newbury
driving twin screws; 211NHP.
Complement: 24 passengers, 52 crew.
11.1929: Completed by Grangemouth
Dockyard Co. Ltd., Grangemouth (Yard No.
416) for Christmas Island Phosphate Co.
Ltd., London as ISLANDER.
1949: Sold to Commonwealth of Australia,
Canberra (British Phosphate Commissioners,
managers), London and Melbourne.
1954: Sold to Christmas Island Phosphate
Commission (British Phosphate
Commissioners, London and Melbourne,
managers).
3.5.1960: Arrived at Hong Kong to be
broken up by Hong Kong Chiap Hua
Manufactory Co. (1947) Ltd.
25.5.1960: Work began.

Tri-ellis at Lyttelton, New Zealand (top) and near Port Chalmers on 22nd February 1976 as *Tryphena* after her sale to the Government of Nauru (middle). *[Ian J.Farquhar; J. and M. Clarkson collection]*

Islander was managed from 1949 until sale for demolition in 1960. *[Russell Priest]*

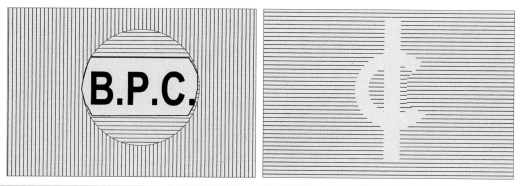

The houseflag of the British Phosphate Commissioners had a red ground with a blue/white/blue ball (near right). The ships had yellow funnels with blue tops. The flag of the Christmas Island Phosphate Co. Ltd. was basically blue (far right). Its funnel was plain yellow. *[J.L. Loughran]*

PUTTING THE RECORD STRAIGHT

Letters, additions, amendments and photographs relating to features in any issues of 'Record' are welcomed. Letters may be lightly edited. Note that comments on multi-part articles are consolidated and included in the issue of 'Record' following the final part. Senders of e-mails are asked to include their postal address.

Smiley's people

Following the references to Hugh Smiley in the William Robertson book and Ships in Focus 'Record' 49, I can add the following.

Sir Hugh Houston Smiley (1841-1909) was born in Larne and lived at his family home, Drumalis House, with its extensive grounds overlooking the entrance to Larne Harbour. He died on 1st March 1909 and is buried in the local cemetery with a large boulder and a plaque marking the grave. Drumalis House is now a convent. Like many other well-off Victorian gentlemen he believed in putting some of his wealth back into the community and was a great benefactor to the town and also like many of his peers he had extensive interests in industry and shipping. His shipping interests later evolved into Howdens shipping company.

The Smiley family first came to Larne from Lanarkshire in 1720 and, like many Ulster folk, maintained a strong Scottish connection. Much of Hugh's wealth was a consequence of his marriage to Elizabeth Kerr from Gallowglass, Paisley, in 1874. She was an only child and heiress to substantial wealth from her family's involvement in the manufacture of sewing thread.

Although there were a number of ship owners based in Larne it was never a port of registry so Shamrock Shipping, Howdens' and Rainey's vessels, amongst others, were mainly registered at Belfast. It is likely because of his wife's connections that Hugh Smiley registered his vessels at Paisley.

The names of the fleet have even closer associations with Larne than Ian Wilson suggests. Olderfleet and Latharna are not merely *near* Larne, they *are* Larne. Olderfleet is a district of Larne near the harbour and the name is said to derive from Ulrik's Fjord after the first Viking settlers there. (I lived in Olderfleet for ten years). Latharna is the Gaelic name for Larne and means the land of Latharn, an ancient local prince. Dalriada is an ancient Celtic kingdom that spanned both North Antrim and large parts of Western Scotland, the choice of name possibly reflecting the marriage of Hugh and Elizabeth from opposite sides of the Irish Sea. The inhabitants of Dalriada were the Scotii (Scots), originally an Irish tribe from County Antrim and through the Kingdom of Dalriada migrated across to what is now modern Scotland

and eventually gave it its name.
JIM MCFAUL, 92 Armorial Road, Styvechale, Coventry CV3 6GJ.
Hugh Smiley is also briefly mentioned in the article on Howdens of Larne in 'British Shipping Fleets 2'.

Clipper reefer origins

Further to the article on the Clipper family of reefer vessels by Tony Breach in 'Records' 47 to 49, I would like to add some details on the inception of the class of what in this country is usually referred to as the 'Drammen reefers'.

The true origin of the class lies, however, with Marinens Hovedverft – the Naval Dockyard at the Karljohansvern naval base in the small town of Horten on the western shore of the Oslofjord. As the naval base was moved to Bergen in 1962 the dockyard underwent a 'civilianization' process and was eventually renamed Horten Verft in 1968.

The shipyard had been heavily involved in the adaptation, design and construction of the five Dealy-class frigates for the Royal Norwegian Navy from 1962. The extent of design and engineering was substantial and the vessels emerged as the *Oslo* class in 1966/67.

Turning its attention to the commercial market from the mid-1960s, the shipyard became involved in a project with Gotaas-Larsen Inc., New York, for the design and construction of two fast reefers. The head of the design office at Horten, Hjalmar Torsteinson, and Knut Børseth of the project division, were instrumental in the design. The hull design was determined after extensive tank testing in Trondheim in 1966 and 1967.

The first vessel *Golar Freeze*, yard number 164, was handed over on 3rd October 1968 and achieved 23.78 knots on trials, propelled by a Sulzer 9RD68 engine, licence-built by the shipyard. However, as the Horten yard by now had a series of bulk carriers on order from H. Hogarth and Sons Ltd., Glasgow, it was decided to transfer the second vessel and leave the design package to Drammens Slip & Verksted, on the condition that the engine of this and future orders should be built at Horten.

This is what happened. The first two, *Golar Freeze* from Horten and *Golar Nel* from Drammen, were built to the original design with flush deck, whereas the subsequent vessels were built to the modified Drammen design.

The origin with the Naval Dockyard by the same people who had been leading the Oslo-class programme may explain the clean and almost martial design of what came to be known as the Clipper reefers.
DAG BAKKA Junior, Haugeveien 31, N-5005 Bergen, Norway

Newbigin plus

Assuming that the vessel inboard of *Grive* ('Record' 51, page 157) had a black funnel with white band on which was a black plus sign, it may have been owned by E.R. Newbigin, Newcastle-upon-Tyne. At the time of the photograph (circa 1908-1910?), Newbigin owned *Greenbatt* (1,407/1908), *Gripfast* (1,109/1910) and *Heworth* (1,043/1900). *Ancient Briton* (1,003/1882) and *Lindisfarne* (1,151/1870) were also earlier members of the fleet.

Readers with access to London arrival/sailing lists of the period may be in a position to confirm or deny.
RICHARD PRYDE, 4 Portlight Close, Mistley, Manningtree, Essex CO11 1UD

Missing Maids

Thank you for Mr Winser's article ('Record' 48 and 49), but what ever happened to the two wonderful *Maid of Orleans*, built by Denny in 1918 and 1949?
D.N. SAUNDERS, 67 George Gurr Crescent, Folkestone, Kent
As John Winser made clear in his introduction to these articles, his intention was to highlight the main phases of development of the railway-owned, cross-Channel vessel and not to provide comprehensive coverage. Ed.

From ships to sandwiches

To be pedantic, the *Nile* (page162, 'Record' 51) is a barque not a ship. The *Celtic* (page 164) was the first ship to exceed the tonnage of the *Great Eastern*; the *Oceanic* (1899) exceeded her length but not her tonnage.

Andrew Bell's hungry midshipmen article in 'Record' 51 revived memories. During the early 1960s Blue Funnel employed the same horrible cheese - I have a sneaking suspicion it was actually Sunlight soap. One of those chartroom cheese sandwiches by 4 in the morning in the Red Sea in August was something to behold - beads of sweat stood out from the cheese and the corners turned up like the roof on a pagoda. During my first watch with the third officer on my first voyage I noticed the chartroom sandwiches and democratically thought half must be mine and acted accordingly. The third officer soon informed me of the enormity of my sin. The galley was locked up like the Bank of England at night but there was a key in the chartroom as the galley provided access to the gyro-room which was checked at the change of the watch,

Gripfast, one of the vessels referred to by Richard Pryde, on her way up the Ouse to Goole to load. Completed by J. Crown at Sunderland in 1910 she was bombed and sunk in July 1944. *[J. and M. Clarkson collection]*

Maid of Orleans of 1918 (above) and her namesake of 1949 (below on trials) were both built by Willliam Denny at Dumbarton. The 1918-built vessel, ordered by the Southern, Eastern and Chatham Railway Company, was torpedoed and sunk on 28th June 1944 whilst on a voyage from the Normandy beachhead to Southampton. The second vessel was built for the British Transport Commission, which later became the British Railways Board, and lasted until 1975 when she was broken up in Spain. *[World Ship Society Ltd.; Newall Dunn collection]*

but nothing was left out in the galley. One could always make toast in the seaman's mess; add to that one's weekly tin of condensed milk and some cocoa powder and you had a very satisfying 'conny-onny and cocoa sandwich'! Salmon sandwiches were provided to the bridge during Suez transits, and only then. Legend had it that in an earlier age somebody called out – what's in the sandwiches? Pork yelled the mid. PORT yelled the quartermaster and drove the ship into the bank. The Marine Superintendent in his wisdom decreed that salmon could not be mistaken for a helm order. Besides, in this day and age a pork sarnie would be inhospitable in Egypt.

The photo of the oily *Neleus* brought back memories too. The engine room in those ships was two frame spaces shorter than in the motor ships. We had an oil spill abreast number 4 hatch at Aden on the *Theseus* - I was sounding the port side, a new Chinese 'chippy's mate' sounding the starboard when a geyser of oil shot out of his sounding pipe over which he had his hands pressed. Oil over the side was one thing (there wasn't pollution then) but the centrecastle deck was sheathed with Borneo cedar and that was a mess. The deck was lovingly barbarized regularly by the crowd and mids (and anyone feeling delicate at 05.30 was completely sober by breakfast time). Returning to the food - it was generally superb and I always felt duty bound to go right through the menu every meal to express my appreciation to the catering crew.

Captain Kinghorn's 'Boxboat Voyage' was evocative too. I recall similar pilot ladders that were a problem. This was in Canadian Pacific's *H.R. McMillan* where the problem was compounded by the hull having an outward flare that the pilots hated. This ship was essentially a large motorised biscuit tin fitted with three gantry cranes. Outbound in ballast, bulk phosphate from Florida to British Columbia, forest products home: I couldn't complain about the hard work; it was worse, it was boring. Consequently I left cargo ships and spent the next 37 years in smaller ships - offshore oil, towing, oceanographic research. The fundamental difference was instead of transiting the seas to work in port, the work was at sea which I found enjoyable.
CAPTAIN JOHN M. ANDERSON, 523 Louise Road, Ladysmith, British Columbia, Canada V9G 1W7

Allied war coaster corrections
I managed to find corrections to the Allied War Coasters article in 'Record' 52.
Adjutant was ex *Myrtlepark* in 1924 not 1922 (page 256).
Uskside was salvaged and became Italian *Teseo* (page 259).
Corfirth was not a total loss; she was salvaged and not scrapped until 1967 (page 260).
LENNART HAGBJER, Kumla Byvag 8, S-17975, Ska, Sweden

Union-Castle R-ships
Having served as the radio officer for two round-trips to the Cape and one round-Africa voyage on *Richmond Castle* (2) followed by two round-trips to the Cape on *Rustenberg Castle* I was most interested in the articles on Union-Castle R-ships in 'Record' 51 and 52 (I don't recall that we ever referred to them as reefers in those days). I have a couple of additional comments which might be of interest.

The change in mast, derricks and derrick-post colour occurred in about 1956 soon after Clan Line took control of Union-Castle. Prior to that masts were all a brown 'mast' colour, but thereafter were changed to white. This change was also applied to the mail and intermediate ships. It was considered a retrograde step by many Union-Castle staff.

The lower picture on page 215 of *Rowallan Castle* was, I am fairly certain, not taken in Cape Town. With the benefit of local knowledge I was not able to recognize any of the background, but the fact that the ship is not flying a courtesy flag at the foremast is confirmation that the photograph was probably taken in the U.K.

The reason that *Riebeeck Castle* is dressed overall is that she was leaving Cape Town on her final voyage. Her long paying-off pennant can be seen hanging down from the port foremast cross-trees (the courtesy flag is to starboard). In Peter Newall's 'Union-Castle Fleet History', there is on page 181 a colour photograph which must have been taken from the same spot but approximately three seconds before the picture in your collection. The former has the caption '*Riebeeck Castle* final sailing in 1971'. Incidentally, in your photo the mast and top of funnel of the 'up-coast' mail ship *S.A. Vaal* ex-*Transvaal Castle* can just be seen above the after end of *Riebeeck Castle's* forecastle.

Rustenburg Castle. [Roy Fenton collection]

I am intrigued by the large number of flags used to dress the ship over-all. Most ships' signal flag lockers had 25 alphabetical flags, 10 numeral pennants, an answering pennant and three substitute flags, so someone must have made a lot of effort to collect all those used! Also, as the ship is relatively lightly-loaded, she would probably not be sailing for the U.K./Continent with a fruit cargo. Possibly the ship went on up the coast to Durban to complete discharging her outward cargo and then sailed direct to the Far East for breaking up. I wonder whether any of your readers can enlighten us.

Many thanks for a most interesting article.
DAVID WITTRIDGE, 25 Fairlawn Close, Rownhams, Southampton SO16 8DT

I feel I must draw your attention to an error in 'Union Castle Reefers 1935-1971 Part 1' by Alan Mallett ('Record' 51).

In the first paragraph he refers to *Dunedin* as being a Shaw Savill ship which she was not at that particular time; he does not even mention the word 'Albion'. The amalgamation did not take place until much later in 1882. As stated she was built in 1874, one of eight sister ships built for Paddy Henderson's Albion Line; she was the longest by one foot.

I was commissioned to build a model for the New Zealand Meat Board's celebration of 125 years since that epic first successful voyage. I was given a great deal of help by both Ian Farquhar of Dunedin and Malcolm D'Arch of Salcombe. The model is in the Meat Board offices in Wellington.
J.D.R. CARRUTHERS, 1 Roddenbury View, Lane End, Corsley, Warminster, Wiltshire BA12 7PT

I read with interest A. Mallett's 'Union-Castle Reefers 1935-1971 part 2'. I would like to add that a updated version of this class was Royal Mail Line's *Loch Loyal* (sister *Loch Gowan* was a steam ship).
A.D. FROST, 32 Oakfield Close, Sunderland SR3 3RT

David Hodge has taken great delight in pointing out an error that I (and everyone else) missed. On page 21 column 2 under 2.8.1942: *Rochester Castle* arrived in Grand Harbour on 13.8.1942, not 15.8.1942.

BOB TODD, Key Specialist Curator, Historic Photographs and Ships Plans Section, National Maritime Museum, London

Reading the letters in 'Record' 51 I was greatly amused by the one from K. Garrett regarding professional rivalry. I assume it was written tongue in cheek. Otherwise if he ever went out on a dark night that he would have to keep looking over his shoulder in case there was an ex-member of the real 'premier company trading to India' waiting to exact his revenge!

In my voyages to the Sub-Continent in the late forties and fifties I cannot remember seeing any Brocklebank vessels, no doubt because the major companies trading out there, besides the Clan Line, were B.I., Bank Line, and Ellermans. As for the 'nine month trips to Calcutta', I presume this must have been under sail, as checking through my Discharge Book, all voyages to India/Pakistan, East Africa or South Africa were in the range of four to five months, from signing on to signing off.

I'm afraid that the writer of the letter should have joined the Scottish Navy and not bothered about yarns of 'the Grey Funnel Line, P&O or the Merchant Navy'. In my humble opinion Clan Line was one of the best shipping companies afloat both for their vessels and their treatment of their crews.

However, as the writer of the letter states 'we all thought our own company was the best', I notice he doesn't say what the outcome was when he refused to join a Clan boat. I can assure him that if he had joined, he would not have found it such a cultural shock as I did, when with the ink still wet on my brand new masters certificate, I joined a Union Castle cargo vessel as a relieving second mate.
BRIAN W. HOLLMAN, 76 Augusta Drive, Augusta Place, Sunningdale, 7441 South Africa

abc of ABCs
I must say how much I enjoyed the 'off the wall' article on the Ian Allan ABC books in Record 50. It set me delving through my bookcase and aroused some happy memories. Somewhat intrigued by the data in your tabulated columns - I

Loch Loyal. [Ships in Focus]

set about examining the volumes I possess- and here's where it all gets rather sad! But I suppose true to its title I offer the following pedantic comments for inclusion in a future 'Putting the Record Straight'.

'British Ocean Liners' (with photo of *Empress of Britain* on cover): the column 2 date should be 1961 (not 1962) - as per page 1 (incidentally page 4 erroneously captions the front cover as showing R.M.S. *Oriana*!)

'British Ocean Tankers' (with photo of *Athelfoam* on cover): the column 2 date should be 1961 (not 1962) - as per page 1.

'Coastal Passenger Ships' (with photo of *Maid of Orleans* on cover): column 2 should show '5th edition' - as per page 1 - and the date should read January 1963 - as per page 3.

'Foreign Ocean Tankers' (with photo of Ditlev-Simonsen tanker on cover): the column 2 date should be 1961 (not 1962) - as per page 1. The photo depicts Ditlev-Simonsen's *Varvara* of 1955 - full details of vessel are given in fleet list on page 14.

'ABC British Tugs' (4th edition with photo of *Maplegarth* on cover): column 2 should also include the date of February 1965 - as per page vi.

NIGEL BOWKER, 9 Boulton Green Close, Bebington, Cheshire.

Nice one, Cyrillic

Received 'Record' 52 today - and I note the subsequent lives of *Brunshoeft* and *Brunstor*. On page 248 you have a photo of each and as a Cyrillic reader with a long ago passed Russian O level, I hope I can help as the caption says it is not possible to tell them apart

The middle photo on page 248 is *Dneprovskiy Liman* - the Cyrillic is clear and her fishing fleet number KT-0270 is clearly marked on the side of the accommodation. This ship's call sign was UTQG and the fishing vessels and their affiliated reefers always had their international call signs painted in the English alphabet on the bridge - usually above the wheelhouse doors on each side. Hard to say conclusdively but the call sign here looks like what it is supposed to be

Likewise, the bottom photo has a fishing number KT-0271 - consecutive to the other vessel indicating they joined the Kaliningrad fishing fleet at the same time (KT is a Kaliningrad code - a bit like GY for Grimsby and PD for Peterhead). This is pretty definitely the *Dnestrovskiy Liman* - her callsign was UTAQ just partially visible above the wheelhouse door. It is impossible to read any name on the hull - but I'd stake a fair bit of wages that this is the former *Brunshoeft*.

BARRY STANDERLINE, Broxy Cottage, 32 North Latch Road, Brechin, Angus DD9 6LE

Thanks also to Richard Pryde for making the same points as Barry and to Colin Menzies for pointing out that identity numbers were used by the USSR to identify vessels associated with fishing, including reefers. Ed.

Archiving

In John Lingwood's article in 'Record' 52 he mentions that the Cleet and Parry operations came to and end when aerial photography took over. This

was done by Turner's Photography in Newcastle. Turner' collection (not only ships) is now owned by Tyne and Wear Archives.

I am a part time volunteer there and am currently compiling a database of the thousands of ship photographs, a task which will take me until a least mid-summer to complete. The collection deals with Sunderland-built ships, from about 1948. As you can imagine there are some superb photos, which should have a wider audience. The Archive staff are currently also cataloguing the archives of the various Sunderland shipbuilders, again another huge task.

IAN RAE, 196 Broadway, Tynemouth, Tyne and Wear NE30 3RY

Plymouth Freighter

It is not quite correct that *Plymouth Freighter* ('Record' 52 page 232) dropped out of 'Lloyd's Register' in 1938, or if she did she was re-entered by the 1940 issue as *Tenace* of the Société Transports Maritime de la Seine Basse, Le Havre. I have her linked to X.210 on the basis that she was one of the 200-225 series which were 105.5 feet compared with the 98 feet of the earlier ones, although 'Lloyd's Register' grants her a length of 100.8 feet, possibly the difference between LP and LOA. In which case, Dobson's X.209, X.211 and X.212 are accounted for, leaving X.210 as the likely culprit. I also have a note of her being sunk in 1942, but regret having lost the source of that titbit, as often happens!

I have updated her entry in the full X-lighter listing on the Clyde Maritime website under http://clydemaritime. co.uk/x210

GEORGE ROBINSON, Southwood Cottage, Southwood Road, Cottingham, East Yorkshire HU16 5AJ

ED follow-up follow-up

I was very pleased to learn that the Elder Dempster series had such a positive reader response. The annual Elder Dempster pensioners' lunch last week learned that the two Liverpool Universities and the Maritime Museum are seeking some lottery funding for an ED archive on the lines of one recently produced for a local post-industrial community. It will be a combination of oral and pictorial evidence including ephemera which will be then professionally interpreted, further correcting the long-standing impression locally that Liverpool only produced one shipping line of importance to its maritime history!

Many thanks for using my recollections in the follow-up. Just one very minor point: the text just below

Identity number KT-0271 clearly identifies this as *Dnestrovskiy Liman*.

half-way on the right-hand column of page 237 mentions 'big vans' in the deep tanks. This should be 'lift vans', those large boxes made of fairly fragile plywood that were used to case up personal and household effects.

As usual, there's always something unexpected and additionally pleasurable in every issue of 'Record'. On this occasion it was those two photographs on page 220 of the *Rakaia*. This was my first ship and the upper picture was taken just two days after completing my first year in that ship. We were inbound from Noumea in New Caledonia, as I recall. You can see from the position of the Plimsoll Line (note its smart white box!) that the MANZ trade was a one-sided one. Apart from a small fleet of Caterpillars for Noumea, our cargo was principally hogsheads of Virginia tobacco, American cars and cased vehicles for General Motor's Holden's assembly plants. We had left Liverpool at the end of February 1959, missed all of that glorious summer and returned to the Mersey at the end of November. At least we had that Christmas at home!

Your choice of pictures, however, always tell a story for those who can look and remember. In the upper view, note that the after lifeboat on the starboard side is swung out. This was our so-called 'accident boat' which could be (and was) used to convey casualties to our resident surgeon. I suspect that it's being readied on this occasion to be put in the water to allow for a run up the river should we be berthed starboard-side alongside. In the lower view (which must date from after 1968) the ship is now just a plain cargo carrier and carries a conventional lifeboat as well as a rather mucky overside that certainly would not have been tolerated in her cadet ship role!
JOHN GOBLE, 55 Shanklin Road, Southampton SO15 7RG

Inadvertently left out of the catalogue of Elder Dempster Lines' post-Second World War cargo ships (Records 47 to 49) were the *Patani* and the *Perang*. This was probably because they were a pair of the most forgettable ships ever built for the company. The story goes that, so shocked were the management at the cost over-runs of the *Eboe* and the *Ebani*, both delivered in 1952, that the building berth for the third ship of the class was used to build a ship whose design closely resembled one of Henderson's numerous 'K' class. With Henderson's UK-Burma trade contracting, most of their general purpose, 9,000 deadweight cargo ships were permanently time chartered to Elder Dempster. The lay out of the two 'P's was similar to the Lithgow-built *Kindat* and *Koyan* but with more substantial cargo gear.

The order for the *Perang* went to William Gray and Co. Ltd. of Hartlepool, not a yard used to Elder Dempster's custom and probably because, amongst a clutch of orders for single ships by a diverse group of ship owners, there was a spare building berth available at short notice. Both 'P' class ships were powered by four-cylinder Doxford-Scotts diesels rated at 2,800 BHP and, on a calm sea passage, could produce a speed of an embarrassingly slow 11 knots. Delivered in 1954 by Scotts and 1955 by Grays, they were the last Elder Dempster ships to have steam-driven winches. In an attempt to get the boiler's smoke clear of the ships, the height of their funnels was raised in 1964.

Their confidence restored, the Elder Dempster directors ordered the third of the E class from Scotts in 1953; she emerged as the *Egori* in 1957.

In 'Record' 47 I wrote that the galley's electrical equipment on the 'P's could not be used when the 'electric' cargo winches were in use. James Cowden corrects me by saying that this was the case when the ship's radar was in use!
ANDREW BELL, 'Gartul', Porthleven, Helston, Cornwall TR13 9JJ

The Lithgows-built, 3,312gt *Patani* was delivered in September 1954 (above), and her funnel was modified in 1964 (below). Following sale to Hong Kong owners in 1972 she was renamed with a few brush strokes as *Patwari*. She reached Gadani Beach for demolition in February 1978. [*J. and M. Clarkson; Malcolm Cranfield*]

The 3,439gt West Hartlepool-built *Perang* was delivered in December 1954 with the short funnel shown in the top photograph. In 1964 this was heightened and the ungainly bits seen in the middle photograph were added. She was sold to Greek owners as *Agnic* in June 1972, and broken up on Gadani Beach during 1978. The top photograph was taken at Boston, U.S.A., the middle photo shows her sailing from Avonmouth on 26th June 1966 and the bottom, as *Agnic,* anchored off Apapa, Lagos on 4th January 1976. *[Malcolm Cranfield; Roy Fenton collection; Malcolm Cranfield]*

Following the discussion of torpedo nets in 'Record' 51 (page 194), Florent Van Otterdyk kindly sent these scans of the nets on the Liberty *Samwater*.

BOSUN'S LOCKER

In this issue we have the luxury of a little over two pages and, having had little space in the last two issues, the old bosun has a few bits and pieces on the shelf in his tagarene shop ranging from information on past photos, a couple of new photos for identification and sadly, an obituary. So, without further ado, let's crack on.

Photo 51/01
Bertil Palm is to be congratulated in identifying the photograph of the wrecked steamer at Eastham in 'Record' 51, which was wrongly named as *Canada*. In fact it shows *Canadia* of Rederi A/B Svenska Lloyd, Göteborg which grounded just outside the entrance to the Manchester Ship Canal on 23rd December 1919 when the line from her tug broke. She became a constructive total loss, as the photograph indicates. The 1,558 grt *Canadia* had been built in 1882 by William Pickersgill and Sons, Sunderland as the *Longueil* for Morel Brothers of Cardiff. In 1897 she was sold to owners in Stettin and was renamed *Albert Köppen*. She passed to Sweden as *Canadia* in 1909, and was bought by Svenska Lloyd in 1916.

Two photographers: an appeal
Tragically, the work of a number ship photographers disappears after they die as families either do not value the photographs, or do not know what to do with them. Phil Thomas was active on the Clyde until quite recently, but a number of enquiries have failed to discover where his negatives ended up. Phil contributed a number of articles to model shipbuilding magazines, and wrote several books published by Charles Waine. Charles does not know what happened to Phil's photos, and neither does the Ballast Trust, a well-known custodian of Scottish photographs. Can anyone help?

Photographs of steamers owned by the Ipswich millers R. and W. Paul Ltd. are particularly elusive, which is a shame as the company is otherwise well documented. Almost all those known are reproduced in Roger Finch's book 'A Cross in the Topsail' (Boydell Press, Ipswich, 1979) which, as its title strongly hints, concentrates on Paul's sailing barges. These photographs are attributed to a J.F. Bear, but it is not known

whether he was a photographer or simply a collector. Does any reader know the whereabouts of Bear's photographs?

J. and C. Harrison
Before moving on to photographs my attention has been drawn to the review in the September 2012 edition of 'Marine News' of our latest publication 'J. and C. Harrison'. The review is generally good. However the reviewer is a little critical of the fleet list section saying that is cramped and difficult to read. We have very good reasons for using a three-column grid. Firstly, many people find that one column on an A4 page is simply too long a line length to read comfortably. With our style, which involves one line per fleet list date, this would also be wasteful of space. A two-column layout is better, but – if photographs are sized to match the columns – this limits the photograph width to a half or a whole page. Three columns gives much more flexibility, as – depending on the space available and its quality – a photograph can go in across a third, two-thirds or the whole page. In the end, it boils down to personal choice, but our experience of laying out many books convinces us that the three-column grid has a lot going for it.

Photo 53/01. This timber-laden steamer has the funnel colours of Bergen Line, but no name is visible and the photographer left no details on the back. A feature which may aid identification is the long bridge deck, which extends well ahead of the superstructure, and the bulwarks of which are painted white.

Photo 53/02.

Reader Jochen Kemsa supplied this very clear photograph of three steamers in the port of Ingeniero White near Bahia Blanca, Argentina around 1910. Two belong to Hain, that inboard being *Trewyn* of 1903, which became a war loss in 1916. The Hain ship outboard has a long bridge deck, a feature which entered the Hain fleet in 1912, so dating the photograph to 1912 to about 1914. The main question is the identity of the Doxford Turret in the middle, which appears to have a buff funnel.

Photo 53/03.

The identity of the small cargo ship in the Mersey is also sought, undoubtedly one of the regular traders on the Irish Sea. She is probably heading for the landing stage at Birkenhead to unload Irish cattle to the lairage.

In 'Record' we try our very best to fully illustrate all articles. On page 150 of 'Record' 51 we recorded the schooner *Rylands* ending her days at Morecambe as *Moby Dick*. We assumed it would be easy to locate a suitable picutre but this was not so. However these pictures arrived soon after publication. The right hand picture shows her at Falmouth as *Dilipa*. The two bottom pictures are of *Rylands* as *Moby Dick* at Morecambe. The left hand pciture was taken

in the very harsh winter of 1962/1963. *[Michael, John and Linda Pryce]*

For the second part of Union Castle reefers in 'Record' 52 we knew the whereabouts of a good wartime view of *Roxburgh Castle* of 1945 but were unable to obtain a print. It is surprising how often, just after an issue of 'Record' has gone to the printers, that a suitable photo turns up. Such was the case with the *Roxburgh Castle* seen at the top of the opposite page in Australian waters. *[Allan C.Green/State Library of Victoria, H91.108 678]*

Graeme Somner – 1921-2012

As readers of 'Marine News' will know, Graeme Somner died earlier this year. Few can have researched and published so assiduously on the shipping of their native area as Graeme, who was brought up on the east coast of Scotland. Several of his contributions to 'Record' have drawn on his early and sometimes unofficial and hair-raising involvement in ships on the Forth, whilst his books published by the World Ship Society and latterly Ships in Focus have covered the major ship owners of this coast.

Wartime service in the Army took Graeme to Gibraltar, where his knowledge of ships got him a dream of a job distributing mail to the many vessels which called. Post-war he joined the management of BOAC, later British Airways, with whom he was based at Heathrow. Living locally he was in easy reach of the Public Record Office where he was one of the pioneers of using registration documents as a basis for researching ships' histories, and where he was consulted by the administration on aspects on their policy of acquiring merchant shipping records.

Aside from his books, Graeme was probably best known for his long-term stewardship of the World Ship Society's Central Record, being himself a Period Custodian and representing the Record on the Society's Committee. His membership number 18 attested to his long involvement with the Society. After he retired, Graeme moved to the South Coast where he was one of the founder members of the Dorset Branch of the WSS.

Only in the last few years did Graeme have to reluctantly give up his research and writing, in the face of deteriorating health of both himself and his wife Hazel. Graeme and Hazel then moved back to Edinburgh to be close to their son Ian.

For his wisdom, knowledge of ships and research, and his companionable nature, Graeme will be much missed and we at Ships in Focus offer our sincere condolences to Hazel and Ian.

SOURCES AND ACKNOWLEDGEMENTS

We thank all who gave permission for their photographs to be used, and for help in finding photographs we are particularly grateful to Tony Smith, Jim McFaul and David Whiteside of the World Ship Photo Library; to Ian Farquhar, F.W. Hawks, Peter Newall, William Schell; and to David Hodge and Bob Todd of the National Maritime Museum, and other museums and institutions listed.

Research sources have included the Registers of William Schell and Tony Starke, 'Lloyd's Register', 'Lloyd's Confidential Index', 'Lloyd's Shipping Index', 'Lloyd's War Losses', 'Mercantile Navy Lists', 'Marine News', 'Sea Breezes' and 'Shipbuilding and Shipping Record'. Use of the facilities of the World Ship Society, the Guildhall Library, the National Archives and Lloyd's Register of Shipping and the help of Dr Malcolm Cooper are gratefully acknowledged. Particular thanks also to Heather Fenton for editorial and indexing work, and to Marion Clarkson for accountancy services.

Brunshausen reefers
Sources include 'The Motorship'; Kludas, A and Witthohn, Ralph 'Die Deutschen Kuhlschiffe'; Hooke, Norman 'Modern Shipping Disasters 1963-1987'; and brokers' lists from Klaveness and Hinrichsen.

Bartram tramps of the thirties
Published sources: 'British Ships Lost at Sea 1939-1945'; Burrell, David 'Scrap and Build'; 'Fairplay Annual Summary of British Shipping Finance' (various years); Foustanos, George M. '100 & 7'; Jenkins, J.Geraint 'Evan Thomas, Radcliffe'; Kulukundis, Manuel E. 'Ships Loved and Painted'; Middlemiss, N.L. 'Travels of the Tramps'; Muckle, W. 'Naval Architecture for Marine Engineers'; Sawyer, L. and Mitchell, W. 'The Empire Ships'; Thomas, P.N. 'British Ocean Tramps'; articles in Ships in Focus 'Record' by Alan McClelland (1) and by Jack Winn (as editor) and John Hill (16).

Gordon Sheves – Fraserburgh shipowner
This article is the work of Graeme Somner with some additional input from the editorial staff. A much shorter version appeared under Graeme's name in the March 1962 'Marine News', but without photographs.

RECORD REVIEWS

BELFAST-BUILT SHIPS
By John Lynch
245 x 170mm softback of 304 pages
Published by The History Press, Stroud, at £19.99.

The cluster of publishers around Stroud (some or all associated with Alan Sutton) have had a reputation for flooding the market with books whose cheapness is often all too apparent in terms of editorial competency and pictorial content. More recently The History Press has partially redeemed this reputation by publishing material which otherwise might never have been made available. However, its extensive output over a broad range of topics means that a reviewer needs to ask how well the author and the potential buyer have been served by this publisher.

The concept of 'Belfast Built Ships' is sound: cover all ships built by the three yards situated in the city. The largest of these, Harland and Wolff, has been chronicled in that monumental tome by Moss and Hume, 'Shipbuilders to the World'. The detailed work of these shipping and industrial historians is unlikely to be bettered, and the author wisely does not try. He does attempt some historical analysis, in suggesting quite plausibly how Belfast builders managed to attract skilled workers from elsewhere (because the town offered opportunities for their wives and daughters to work in the linen industry). Less convincing is his analysis of why Harland and Wolff were so successful, attributing this largely to their relationship with companies in the Kylsant group, and neglecting such factors as their early embrace of diesel engine technology.

With Workman, Clark, one could wish for a fuller account of the business as, to this reviewer's knowledge, no detailed history of this important middle-sized yard has appeared in print. The history of the third Belfast yard, McIlwaine and Lewis (later McIlwaine and McColl), gets little more than a page.

As the title indicates, the emphasis is on the ships themselves, and this is reflected in chapters exploring the output of Belfast yards by period, and telling the stories of selected ships. In the latter chapter, entitled 'Urban Myths and Forgotten Histories', the author rightly laments the vastly disproportionate attention lavished on Harland and Wolff's unfortunate yard number 401, but spends a disproportionate number of pages doing so.

Illustrations comprise some good views of the two main yards and representative vessels (the latter often presented rather small), with several pages of rather simplistic profile drawings of representative ships, all to different scales. Much better to have devoted these pages to more, or just larger, photographs.

It seems the author is determined to tell his story largely in terms of statistics, and tables dominate the book. The major ones record launchings in Belfast by year, provide an alphabetical list of locally-built ships, and tabulate each yard's output in detail. The author attempts to improve on Moss and Hume's yard list of Harland and Wolff by providing additional detail of the careers of the ships. For this yard and for Workman, Clark, the major source of such detail is almost certainly the Miramar Index. Where this does not provide the necessary detail, especially in the case of the McIlwaine yard's output of coastal ships, the errors multiply and become unacceptable. Names are mis-spelt far too often to be accidental typos, and ships' careers are incompletely explored or mixed up. For instance, the career of *Parkmore*, McIlwaine and Lewis' yard number 10, certainly did not end after her collision in 1914: she was salved and served for another 11 years. Worse, yard number 11, *Topic* of 1881 which became *Volga* in 1888, is treated as two distinct ships (one with the fictitious yard number 12) and no fate is recorded for her (she was broken up in 1937). Amongst many mis-spellings Langlands become Manglands, *Glenariff* becomes *Glanariff*, *Stangarth* is repeatedly rendered *Strangarth*, the town of Dumbarton is invariably spelt Dunbarton, builders Bartrams are named as Bartrains, and a Sunderland shipbuilder is referred to as 'Bulmens' which is presumably Blumers. Should the reviewer be accused of pedantry here, he would cite the author's own pedantry. He repeatedly corrects Moss and Hume's description of vessels as 'passenger ships' maintaining that they are 'passenger-cargo ships', blind to the former being the accepted term and to the fact that very few ships built by Harland and Wolff could ever be regarded as 'pure' passenger ships.

The book certainly has merit in cataloguing the output of all three Belfast shipyards and represents a formidable amount of work. But it is let down by the all-too-numerous errors, which reduce confidence in the remainder, and by the weakness of the business histories of the yards. The author of such a detailed and ambitious work would have been better served by a specialist publisher who could have provided better guidance and a more critical appraisal of its factual content.

Roy Fenton

IRISH SEA SCHOONER TWILIGHT: THE LAST YEARS OF THE WESTERN SEAS TRADERS
By Richard J. Scott
275 x 215mm hardback of 184 pages
Published by Black Dwarf Publications, Lydney, at £24.99

Richard Scott of Limerick, who died in 2008, was an enthusiast for, writer about and photographer of the small wooden sailing vessels which hung on in Irish Sea trades, and usually in Irish ownership, until the 1960s. From 1945 he spent working holidays on these craft, developing a deep knowledge of the vessels themselves and the men who owned and crewed them. His writing on these craft is rich in atmosphere and anecdote, but he also recorded the details of how so many of them met melancholy and usually violent ends.

This book has had a somewhat chequered history, Ships in Focus being at one time involved but having it withdrawn by Scott's family. Our experience indicated that, although the text was sound, like most books it needed competent subediting, and this it has had from those involved with Black Dwarf Publications. Seven chapters cover aspects of the trade of various ports where the craft were owned or, in the case of the *Brooklands* and *Kathleen and May* on which Scott sailed, detailed accounts of their history, equipment, crews and voyage patterns. An eighth chapter records losses from 1918 to 1934. These cut off dates are somewhat arbitrary, but the editors generously note that Martin Benn's 'Closing Down Sail' provides a definite list of coastal sailing ship losses. The long Chapter 9 provides brief details of most of the British and Irish sailing craft which survived in 1935, with in many cases an indication of their fate. There are four appendices which cover the voyages of the *Susan Vittery*, list the Irish and North Devon fleets in 1910, and detail the cargoes carried by Irish schooners during the Second World War, plus a bibliography and indexes of people, companies and ships. The only minor niggle which this reviewer has with the text – and one by no means confined to this book – is the unnecessary use of 'MV' or 'SS' for the fully-powered coasters mentioned, which results in such tautologies as '...his ship MV *Firth Fisher*'.

In fact, the text – good as it is – is perhaps secondary to the photographs, the majority taken by Scott himself and depicting the vessels, their gear and crew in often intimate detail. Reproduction of these is exemplary, a credit to both those who prepared them for publication and the printers, Berforts of Eynsham. It is only a shame that, in trying to make use of some of the best photographs, the designer has spread them across two pages with the inevitable result that the gutter, and its white space, distracts from the image's impact.

Editors, publishers and printers are to be congratulated in turning Richard Scott's words and photographs into the book they richly deserve, at a reasonable price for such a quality production. It even has a dust jacket: a luxury in today's maritime publishing environment.

Roy Fenton